On the rationality of borrowers' behaviour

Comparing risk attitudes of homeowners

The series **Sustainable Urban Areas**
is published by IOS Press under the imprint Delft University Press

IOS Press BV
Nieuwe Hemweg 6b
1013 BG Amsterdam
The Netherlands
Fax +31-20-6870019
E-mail: info@iospress.nl

Sustainable Urban Areas is edited by
Delft Centre for Sustainable Urban Areas
C/o OTB Research Institute for Housing, Urban and Mobility Studies
Delft University of Technology
Jaffalaan 9
2628 BX Delft
The Netherlands
Phone +31 15 2783005
Fax +31 15 2784422
E-mail mailbox@otb.tudelft.nl
http://www.otb.tudelft.nl

On the rationality of borrowers' behaviour

Comparing risk attitudes of homeowners

PROEFSCHRIFT

Ter verkrijging van de graad van doctor
aan de Technische Universiteit Delft,
op gezag van de Rector Magificus prof. dr. ir. J.T. Fokkema,
voorzitter van het College voor Promoties,
in het openbaar te verdedigen op maandag 27 oktober 2008 om 12.30 uur
door

Peter NEUTEBOOM

doctorandus in de economie

geboren te Zoetermeer

Dit proefschrift is goedgekeurd door de promotoren:
Prof. dr. P.J. Boelhouwer
Prof. dr. ir. H. Priemus

copromotor
Dr.ir. M.G. Elsinga

Samenstelling promotiecommissie:
Rector Magnificus, voorzitter
Prof. dr. P.J. Boelhouwer, Technische Universiteit Delft, promotor
Prof. dr. ir. H. Priemus, Technische Universiteit Delft, promotor
Dr. ir. M.G. Elsinga, Technische Universiteit Delft, copromotor
Prof. dr. J. Doling, University of Birmingham
Prof. dr. A.H. Kleinknecht, Technische Universiteit Delft
‚Prof. dr. D. Brounen, Erasmus Universiteit Rotterdam
Prof. dr. J.B.S. Conijn, Universiteit van Amsterdam
Prof. dr. W.K. Korthals Altes, Technische Universiteit Delft, reservelid

On the rationality of borrowers' behaviour. Comparing risk attitudes of homeowners, by Peter Neuteboom
Thesis Delft University of Technology, Delft, The Netherlands

The author wishes to acknowledge the financial assistance of the Dutch government through the Habiforum Program Innovative Land Use and Delft University of Technology through the Delft Centre for Sustainable Urban Areas

Design: Cyril Strijdonk Ontwerpbureau, Gaanderen
Dtp: Yvonne Alkemade, Delft
Printed in the Netherlands by: Haveka, Alblasserdam

ISSN 1574-6410; 21
ISBN 978-1-58603-918-9
NUR 755

Legal notice: the publisher is not responsible for the use which might be made of the following information.

Contents

Preface

The ambition to write someday a PhD slumbered for years while I was working at the Dutch Ministry of Housing, Spatial Planning and the Environment. When the opportunity eventually presented itself, the first of many challenges to come was the angle of the research. The theme – the risks of homeownership – was the starting point, but not very precise; not surprisingly it took some time to figure it all out.

This PhD thesis on 'borrowers' behaviour across countries' was prompted by two observations: first, mortgage take-up amongst homeowners was fairly divergent across Europe, and second, that this was seen by academic researchers as well as policymakers and financial authorities as an indication of fundamental differences in the risk attitudes of homeowners. That conclusion seemed at odds with numerous (international comparative) studies, which indicated, that the outcome on a macro level – in this case mortgage take-up – is not necessarily a good indicator of the underlying decision-making process. My research results support the latter view.

Six years later, time was up, meaning that the PhD had to be finished. It took a while to accept that fact; for the same reasons as formulated by Sidney Weintraub in the early 1930s: "I continually hear things ... which leaves me in a muddle, things that I recognize should come in, but which mean that I've got to change my own attack somewhat. But remind me that a doctorate hinges on finishing it. Refinements can come later. Yet, I don't relish working when I'm not certain in my own mind." (Cited by Weintraub, 2002). Therefore, even when this study is finished, I comfort myself with the thought that this thesis is not the end, just an intermediate phase, and a prelude to even more exciting things.

It is traditional in the preface to a PhD thesis to say a word of thanks to many people who have contributed over the years to the research. Many did – in one way or another – but most of them will remain anonymous. Here, I would just like to thank both my (co-)promoters (Peter Boelhouwer, Hugo Priemus and Marja Elsinga), whose critical comments on earlier drafts improved the final version significantly. My wife, Corinne, who kept me grounded when I was euphoric and vice versa. Finally, my son Ernst, who retyped many tables when Gates' brainchild broke down once again (any remaining errors are, of course, mine!).

Peter Neuteboom,
Monday, 7 July 2008

1 Comparing mortgage risks in a cross-country framework

"I often say that when you can measure what you are speaking about and express it in numbers you know something about it; but when you cannot measure it, when you cannot express it in numbers, your knowledge is of a meagre and unsatisfactory kind."
William Thomson, 1855 (cited in Porter, 1995)

1.1 Introduction

Things were hectic on the housing and mortgage markets in the 1990s. Although the time and depth of the cycles differed from one European country to another, by the end of the 1990s homeownership rates had risen and house prices had doubled in most countries (with some notable exceptions), while total outstanding mortgage debt had more than tripled (ECB, 2003). Overall, the influx of new households in the homeownership sector and the increase in the withdrawal of housing equity appeared to have made individual homeowners and the financial sector more vulnerable to economic downturns.

These days, most Europeans are owner-occupiers (64%, Eurostat, 2006). In many countries, homeownership is promoted either directly or indirectly by the government via subsidies, high fiscal support and/or by phasing out support to the rented sector. The deregulation of the financial markets since the 1980s has also pushed up homeownership rates. Homeownership is, however, inseparable from a minimum level of income security (Ford *et al.*, 2002): the purchase of a home is by far the greatest financial commitment that most households ever acquire, while the monthly mortgage payments consume a major part of their net income. To many households, their home is the largest, if not the only, capital asset they possess. Deregulation of the national labour market and changes to the social security system in recent years – due to globalisation and far-reaching integration in the European Union – have, however, weakened the links in the traditional triangle of homeownership, the labour market and the social security system. As a result, homeownership seems to be creating more risks for individual homeowners and society at large.

Meanwhile, even though the mechanisms of insecurity operate in the same way in different countries, the wide variation in mortgage take-up across Europe suggests that individual households (by their attitudes) and governments (by their policies) exert a strong influence. In recent decades, considerable comparative research has been conducted into the operations of the mortgage market in the EU and elsewhere (Diamond and Lea, 1992; Ball and Grille, 1997; Maclennan *et al.*, 1999; Ball, 2003; European Mortgage Federation, 1995, 2003, 2005), which shows that the differences between countries are relatively large *"due to differences in land law, tax law, consumer protection, the financial structure of the capital market and social-cultural differences"* (Bartlett and Bramley, 1994, p. 8). This conclusion has been confirmed by more recent studies on mortgage take-up among owner-occupiers in Europe (ECB, 2003; Mercer

Table 1.1 Some indicators of mortgage take-up by all homeowners, absolute values and, in brackets, rank order (Europe, 2003)

	Outstanding mortgage debt (% GNP)		Loan-to-income ratio		Loan-to-value ratio		Debt-service ratio	
Belgium	28.5	(7)	1.42	(9)	0.54	(7)	0.10	(9)
Denmark	87.5	(2)	3.68	(4)	0.70	(5)	0.12	(8)
France	24.7	(8)	2.64	(6)	0.75	(3)	0.17	(5)
Germany	54.3	(4)	3.00	(5)	0.98	(1)	0.20	(2)
Italy	13.8	(9)	2.52	(8)	0.65	(6)	0.18	(3)
Netherlands	99.9	(1)	4.42	(3)	0.72	(4)	0.13	(7)
Portugal	50.6	(5)	4.75	(2)	--	--	0.23	(1)
Spain	42.1	(6)	4.79	(1)	--	--	0.18	(4)
UK	70.4	(3)	2.54	(7)	0.77	(2)	0.17	(6)

Source: European Central Bank, European Community Household Panel

Debt-service ratio is the ratio of net housing costs to net household income. Ranking order is based on high to low comparison.

Oliver Wyman, 2003, 2005).

Often for the lack of anything better, these differences in mortgage take-up between countries are viewed as indicators of the risks run by individual owner-occupiers, the financial sector and/or the economy as a whole. More implicitly, it is assumed that they reflect an underlying difference in the risk attitudes of owner-occupiers (e.g. ECB, 2003; BIS, 2006). The risk attitude of the more liberal Anglo-Saxon society (supposed to be 'risk-taking') is contrasted with the risk attitude of the continental welfare states (supposed to be 'risk-averse').

However, there is very little systematic evidence to support this assumption (Doling and Ford, 2003); the facts actually point in the opposite direction. This is illustrated in Table 1.1 and Figure 1.1. Table 1.1 shows a number of frequently used macro-indicators for mortgage take-up in nine European countries: the outstanding mortgage debt as a percentage of the gross national product and the estimated loan-to-income ratio, loan-to-value ratio and debt-service ratio of average homeowners, i.e. including outright owners.

Although the ranking differs slightly for each indicator, three groups are clearly distinguishable: Denmark, the Netherlands and the UK make up the leading group (countries with a relatively high mortgage take-up), while Belgium, France and Italy bring up the rear[1]. The other countries – Germany, Portugal and Spain – fill in the middle positions. Note that although the loan-to-income and loan-to-value ratio in Southern Europe are low, the preference of owner-occupiers in these countries for short-term mortgages, long fixed-interest periods and rapid repayment plans means that the debt-service ratio

---

[1] The qualification 'bringing up the rear' is not a-prior negatively intended.

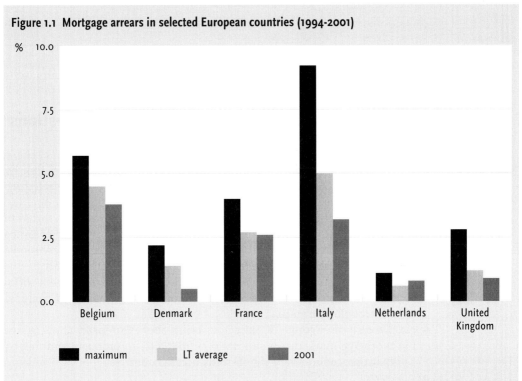

Figure 1.1 Mortgage arrears in selected European countries (1994-2001)

Source: European Community Household Panel

The figure shows the percentage of households with a mortgage that report they were in arrears for more than three months. The maximum and long-term average data is based on the period 1994 to 2001; latest year available – i.e. 2001 – is shown as well. In all countries, the incidence of arrears has decreased over the years in line with the economic cycle over this period.

is relatively high. Figure 1.1 shows the counterbalance of mortgage take-up: the percentage of self-reported arrears[2]. Strikingly enough, the countries with the highest mortgage take-up also have the lowest percentage of arrears. In other words, the link between mortgage take-up and risk does not appear to be very strong.

This first, rather simple, research suggests a rather weak link between mortgage take-up and arrears; it seems therefore that one or more 'unknown' variables are influencing the outcome. Hence, it would be rash to draw conclusions about risks for individuals and society solely based on a number of output indicators such as the loan-to-income ratio or the outstanding mortgage debts in percentage of the gross national product. Clearly, the linkage between mortgage take-up and the underlying risk attitudes of borrowers is even less tough.

2 Risk can be enumerated in many ways, arrears are just one example.

1.2 Problem definition and research questions

Problem definition
What are the likely explanations for this apparently absent, direct link between mortgage take-up and risk for individuals and society? There are three possible candidates:
- The institutional context is different in each country not just with regard to the much-quoted mortgage interest tax relief, but in a wide range of issues, such as consumer protection (e.g. procedures surrounding repossessions) and the level of social security (unemployment benefit, pensions, etc.).
- The characteristics of individual owner-occupiers and borrowers differ considerably between countries (in terms of income, household composition, age, capital formation, etc.).
- Finally, despite vigorous attempts to bring about European convergence, the mortgage markets are still national markets; so products and risk-assessment procedures vary significantly across countries.

These factors – together with mortgage interest rates and developments in net income and property prices during the lifetime of the mortgage contract – exert a strong influence on the expected net costs and risks (ex-ante probability and impact) of taking out a mortgage to finance one's own home, i.e. the risk profile of the mortgage in question. In other words, the risk profile of an identical mortgage contract for €100,000 will be different for Dutch and Italian homeowners. It may therefore be expected that although the chosen mortgage types vary between countries (e.g. in terms of amount and fixed-interest period) the risks need not be all that different. This likewise applies to the underlying risk attitude of owner-occupiers in other EU-countries.

In short, one cannot definitively determine the costs – and, by extension, the risks (and risk attitudes) – that owner-occupiers have undertaken, based on a set of one-dimensional key figures (like the indices in Table 1.1). What is needed in order to draw up an adequate comparison of both the risks and the risk attitude of individual owner-occupiers is *"to quantify the features of national systems in a consistent fashion"* (Oxley, 2001). Without a common denominator, it is impossible to identify, compare or resolve the different risks. Therefore, if we are to draw any conclusions on the risks homeowners are apparently willing to take, we should not concentrate on mortgage take-up as such, but on the net costs and risks it represents to the same homeowners.

Given the multiple nature of the risks and the complexity of the dynamics, transforming mortgage take-up into the costs and risks of mortgages for owner-occupiers will be a complicated affair; certainly in a cross-country framework. This is the challenge at the core of this study. The central problem definition of this thesis is therefore:

How can the risk attitude of borrowers be measured consistently and compared in a cross-country framework?

Many have argued that housing risk is a complex and multifaceted phenomenon, involving many exogenous and endogenous factors, which are unevenly distributed and constantly changing (Lawson, 2005). One way to address the task at hand – comparing the risk attitudes of borrowers across Europe – is to analyse in detail the different factors that influence mortgage costs and which contribute to mortgage risks in different countries, thereby building on the already encyclopaedic knowledge of housing and mortgage markets across Europe. However, as this could easily create an information overload, a more 'reductionist' approach is far more appealing: *"telling the whole story with just a small set of numbers"* (Porter, 1995). Therefore, the general aim of comparing the risks and risk attitudes of mortgages in a European perspective will be pursued within the context of a second aim, namely: to keep things comprehensible. This implies the use of just a small set of indicators to capture the differences and similarities between risks and risk attitudes across countries.

Hypothesis
If mortgage take-up across Europe varies against a background of different institutions etcetera, what can we expect of the underlying risk attitudes of owner-occupiers; i.e. how plausible is it to expect risk attitudes – at country level – to be different across Europe? Rational choice theory[3] states that, under equal circumstances, households will opt for the alternative that they perceive as offering the best (lowest) costs and risks. Under the preconditions of rational choice theory, borrowers maximise a utility function U, which may be defined as:

$$U = U(C,R:X) \quad U_C^1 < 0 \quad U_R^1 < 0$$

where C denotes the expected costs over the full duration of the mortgage (in net present value terms), R the risk associated with that mortgage, while X is a set of factors reflecting household characteristics, economic conditions, institutions and risk attitude. Both C and R depend on the mortgage contract specification (amortisation term, duration, fixed interest period etc.). All borrowers will maximise U over the different mortgage contracts available to them. If payment constraints matter, the borrower will minimise costs. If, however, payment constraints are not binding he will chooses for an option that minimise both costs and (a fraction) of the risks, depending on his risk

---

3 Rational choice theory underpins much of economic theory today, but is well established within other social sciences as well (see Chapter 2 for a further elaboration).

attitude.

If one assumes that households across Europe all have the same level of knowledge of, for instance, the relevant institutions in their own country, and are equally capable of estimating adequately the risks of homeownership[4], then we cannot suppose a-priori that differences in mortgage take-up between countries point to differences of the underlying risk attitudes. That is, the utility maximisation for a borrower is conditional on X, i.e. on household characteristics, economic conditions, institutions and risk attitude. I.e. if mortgage choices are different between homogenous groups of households, this result may be merely a reflection of differences in the underlying institutional context, individual household characteristics and/or the structure of national mortgage markets altering the best mortgage contract for a homeowner.

This thesis will test the following hypotheses:

I. *Households behave rational when choosing a specific mortgage type; i.e. they choose a mortgage that constitute, for them, the lowest costs and/or risks.*
II. *The risk attitude of owner-occupiers with similar individual characteristics is identical across countries when adjusted for differences in institutions and the structure of national mortgage markets.*

The first hypothesis follows directly from rational choice theory. The second hypothesis can be interpreted two-folded[5]. In the weak version of the hypothesis, the expectation is that all households in the different countries are revealing a risk-averse attitude towards mortgage debt, as one may expect given the high financial commitment at stake. In a stronger version of the hypothesis, no significant differences in the risk attitude of owner-occupiers with similar individual characteristics are expected between countries (i.e. when comparing homogeneous groups of households).

The research in this thesis concentrates on differences in mortgage risks and risk attitudes between countries. Although I do not expect risk attitudes to vary between countries, this is not to say that attitudes cannot and will not differ within a country; individual differences in knowledge, perception and attitude are real, but they lapse at a more aggregated level.

Research questions

The above discussion raises five research questions:

1. First how, and to what extent, does mortgage take-up vary in Europe, and

---

4 That is not to say that households have perfect/full knowledge of all the risks. *"Economic agents do not have unlimited information-processing capabilities. It is eminently 'rational' for people to adopt rules of thumb as a way to economize on cognitive faculties"* (Mullainathen and Thaler, 2000, p. 4). The point being argued here is that households in one country are not generally better informed than households in other countries.

5 Implicit in this hypothesis is, of course, the premise that borrowers choose rational (optimal).

to what extent does the relevant context within Europe diverge?

Thereafter the more theoretical/methodological questions:

2. How can the expected costs and risks of a mortgage be quantified for an owner-occupier? And

3. How can this framework be extended to compare the risk attitude of borrowers across countries?

Then, zooming in on the empirical results:

4. Do households, on average, choose the optimal mortgage, i.e. act rationally?

5. To what extent does the risk attitude of homogeneous groups of owner-occupiers differ between countries within Europe?

I will discuss these research questions briefly.

Question 1. A more comprehensive insight needs to be gained into mortgage take-up across Europe, both at macro and micro level. Secondly, the three factors identified before, which can explain differences in mortgage take-up across countries as well as influencing the costs and risks of a mortgage should be analysed. In this thesis, a more descriptive analysis will be undertaken in order to analyse the most important features of mortgage take-up and the relevant context.

Question 2. I shall address this question with a stochastic model in which household income, house prices, inflation, interest rates and so on are represented by a set of stochastic differential equations. In the model the characteristics of individual households and the mortgage are combined with a number of aspects from the institutional context. By generating different scenarios for future developments in, for example, house prices, household income and so on, the model makes it possible to calculate the net mortgage payments, i.e. the net present value of the annual net mortgage payments over the full term of the mortgage for individual homeowners and at a more aggregate level. So, each scenario is supplemented with an outcome. Hence, the net mortgage payments are no longer characterised only by a single, most probable result, but by a probability distribution of all possible results. The average of this distribution is an indication of the expected costs of the mortgage, based on different scenarios; the variation in the results can then serve as the basis for risk determination (Trigeorgis, 1996). This framework can also be applied to different countries and hence different institutional contexts, making it possible to measure the extent to which net costs are influenced by the institutional context.

The model also provides information about the future debt-service ratio, i.e. the ratio of net mortgage payments to net household income. This debt-service ratio can then be used as a trigger for two specific mortgage risks: arrears and repossessions. In other words, a debt-service ratio that rises above a certain time-dependent level may lead to payment arrears, which, if they persist for a longer period, will ultimately lead to repossession. The model allows us to calculate the ex-ante probability of these risks.

Question 3. Previously assessed ex-ante costs and risks are not sufficient for a proper comparison of the risk attitude of owner-occupiers in different countries. Rational choice theory teaches us that households, under identical circumstances, will opt for the alternative that they see as the best deal in terms of costs and returns. If there is any uncertainty in the decision as regards, for example, the future costs or risks of a mortgage, then there is no unequivocal choice; the optimum shifts depending on the risk attitude of the decision-maker. Therefore, to measure the risk attitude of owner-occupiers, it is necessary to consider how the costs and risks (see discussion of research question 2) of their actual choice relate to the costs and risks of all the alternatives available to them within the same institutional context. Then it is possible to see whether the actual choice is optimal and/or the extent to which the owner-occupier chooses an option (i.e. a specific mortgage contract) with a low or high-risk profile. The risk attitude thus measured can then be easily compared in an international framework; the corrections needed for differences in institutions, household characteristics and supply-side limitations have already been discounted in the calculation of the costs and risks, which serve as the basis for deriving the actual risk attitude.

Questions 4/5. In short, do the hypotheses stipulated earlier hold true? If so, what are the implications for scientists and policymakers? In addition, if not, what could account for the differences in risk attitudes?

1.3 Scientific and societal contribution

Scientific contribution

Very few comparative international studies have been carried out in this field to date. Those which have been conducted (see the references above, amongst others) are often descriptive in nature and make a wavering attempt to up-scale the analysis by comparing a number of key figures between countries, studies which Oxley (*ibid.*) calls 'low-level comparative'. Any explicit attention devoted by such studies to the risk of financing one's own home with a mortgage, often consists of an ex-post approach which focuses on scope and/or (social) consequences and remedies for households with payment (and/or repossession) problems; see for instance Ford *et al.* (2002) or Kempson *et al.* (2005).

In a more methodological sense a link is sought with stochastic modelling as applied in mainstream finance theory. Two such studies are important here: Yang *et al.* (1998) and Campbell and Cocco (2003). Both construct stochastic models to illustrate the costs and/or default risks of mortgages and both are crafted on the American context. The model of Yang *et al.* is a simple model for determining the ex-ante probabilities of mortgage default. The model of

Campbell and Cocco is far more elaborate – addressing, amongst other things, income changes at a micro level – but the analysis is limited to determining the expected costs of a mortgage (in the US).

My study differs in a number of respects from the studies quoted above. First, it embodies an international comparison, not of markets and agents, but of the expected net costs and the implied risks of a mortgage for an owner-occupier, while taking account of the institutional differences (to quote Oxley, 'high level comparative'). Secondly, it is an ex-ante approach, which is designed to offer more insight into the underlying risk behaviour, i.e. the risk attitude of owner-occupiers[6]. Thirdly, it is an analysis at intermediate level, which compares sub-categories (e.g. borrowers, recent buyers, first-time buyers, different age categories) in the housing market from an international perspective rather than just the national averages.

Finally, this study focuses on the quantification of risks and risk attitudes. Naturally, this implies an emphasis on the financial risk for owner-occupiers, but that is not to say that expected negative social consequences do not matter; they do – certainly for the individuals concerned. The question is whether these issues shape the risk attitudes of individual homeowners; here I assume that they do not[7].

Societal contribution

The financial authorities in the EU follow developments on the housing and mortgage markets closely. The outstanding mortgage debt at micro level, but also at macro level, is so large that developments in the housing and mortgage market have direct repercussions on the economy as a whole[8]. Sometimes in a positive sense; for example, at the end of the 1990s, economic growth in the Netherlands was strongly driven by rising consumer spending, which was partly influenced by equity growth (DNB, 2002). However, a negative spiral is equally conceivable. See, for instance the present Credit Crisis; here, the housing and mortgage market turbulence in the US has led to a slowdown of the economy[9] (IMF, 2008). At present, financial authorities have to rely on simple macro indicators (like presented in Table 1.1) to monitor developments on the (international) mortgage markets. Then, the high loan-to-value ratios in for instance the Netherlands, worry them, fuelling fear for

---

6 Obviously, given the aim of the study, the starting point is the view of individual homeowners, neither the 'mortgage industry' nor the government. However, the implications of the risk attitudes of individual homeowners are of importance to both the industry and the government.

7 This issue will be further addressed in Chapter 2.

8 Following the introduction of the euro, the economies of European countries have become more intertwined, also in a monetary sense.

9 Although lenders are eager to alter the causal relation; in their view, the slowdown of the economy (recession) is the main cause of the problems on the US housing market and not their lending behaviour.

similar developments in the Netherlands as happening nowadays in the US. However, the likelihood of a downturn of Dutch housing and mortgage markets depends on more factors that can be grasped by a simple comparison of some output indicators (see discussion in Section 1.2). More insight into the actual ex-ante risks of outstanding mortgages is needed; the model developed in this thesis could contribute to this.

Although the model developed in this study is used to compare the net costs and implied risks of mortgage financing by owner-occupiers in a European perspective, it may also be used for other purposes. First, in a more prescriptive sense, it could be used to determine the optimal mortgage in terms of scope and characteristics for individual owner-occupiers, given the household characteristics and the institutional context (checklist of what to choose and what to avoid). Secondly, it can help to estimate the risks in a lender's mortgage portfolio, an area that has gained in importance since the implementation of Basel II.

1.4 Structure of the thesis

In broad terms, the contents of this thesis follow the five research questions formulated in Section 1.2. Chapter 2 expatiates on the theoretical background of risk and risk measurement and leads to a conceptual model that forms the basis for modelling the cost and risk of a mortgage, and subsequently to derive the risk attitude. The description of the context is the central issue in Chapter 3, which analyses the differences and similarities in mortgage take-up in the various countries (at macro and micro level) and the incidence of mortgage arrears and repossessions in Europe. Next, the characteristics of owner-occupiers and institutions are discussed. Finally, this chapter homes in on the structure of the mortgage market, specifically the product variation and borrowers' accessibility. Chapter 4 transforms the conceptual model into a simulation model in which the mortgage costs and risks can be computed for owner-occupiers. A comprehensive description and the results of the model, i.e. the costs and risks in the various countries, are discussed. Chapter 5 develops the model further to measure the risk attitude of households; the method, the results and the robustness of the results are discussed. Finally, Chapter 6 summarises and discusses the – policy and scientific – implications of the findings of this study.

2 On the quantification of mortgage risks

"Nothing is a risk in itself; there is no risk in reality. But on the other hand, anything can be a risk, it all depends on how one analyzes the danger, considers the event. As Kant might have put it, the category of risk is a category of the understanding; it cannot be given in sensibility or intuition." François Ewald, 1991, p. 199.

2.1 Introduction

Increasingly, we are preoccupied with risk management (avoidance) at individual level and risk redistribution at societal level (Beck, 1992). Beck's risk society thesis claims that modern social and economic relationships are more susceptible than ever before to uncertainty, flexibility, and change, and hence are more likely to have negative repercussions on individuals and society.

The issue of risks, whatever their nature, can only be addressed within a framework which enables us to quantify those risks in a manner acceptable to all (or the vast majority). If not, neither communication nor design strategies to handle these risks will be feasible. Therefore, quantification is not merely an (academic) exercise, but a social technology as well (Porter, 1995); it is primarily an attempt to create objectivity, to offer an alternative for subjective (expert) opinions (Croft, 2001). Of course, one can use numbers just as an illustration, but in science and for the broader public, quantification stands for thoroughness and clarity.

This chapter deals with three issues. First, it addresses the concepts of 'risk' and 'risk attitude', all vital issues in this study (Section 2.2). Next, in Section 2.3, the theoretical and empirical literature on mortgage risks is reviewed briefly with the aim of identifying the main drivers of those risks. Finally, some basic, non-technical issues, concerning mortgage risk modelling are discussed, finishing off with an outline of the conceptual model that lies at the basis of the mortgage risk quantification used in this thesis (Section 2.4).

2.2 Conceptualising mortgage risks

The terms 'risk' and 'risk attitude' were somewhat loosely applied in the opening chapter. This section takes a closer look at both concepts and zooms finally in on the relevant mortgage risks taken into account in this study.

Definition of risk

What do we mean when we use the term 'risk'? Usually, this question is answered with a formal definition in which topics like probability, uncertainty, danger, peril, loss etc. all play an important role. A frequently used definition is *".. a numerical measure of the expected harm or loss associated with an adverse event"* (Adams, 1995, quoting the Royal Society). Two things are crucial in this definition: it is about (1) the quantification of (2) some possible negative con-sequence ("harm or loss"). This concept of risk is far apart from notions of uncertainty and hazard, although these latter concepts are – in usage – seen as exchangeable. Uncertainty refers to uncertain outcomes, either positive or negative, while hazard refers to the actual source of danger.

It follows from the definition that risks are, by nature, both calculable and collective (Ewald, 1991). A possible event may only be considered a risk, if it can be expressed in terms of probability. Whether this probability is objective or subjective is irrelevant. If we have no knowledge or idea of the possibility of a specific event or its consequences, we do not use the word 'risk'. Secondly, risks are collective. There is, strictly speaking, no such thing as an individual risk. A risk implies membership of a group. Admittedly, if the risk materialises in the form of, say, an accident or payment difficulties, it manifests itself first and foremost at an individual level, but that does not alter the fact that the probability is determined at a higher, more collective level.

The question – *What do we mean by risk?* – was answered above with a rou-tine definition, but that is not the end of the story. What people see as a risk may not necessarily be imminent. For example, many people consider nuclear energy as a major risk[10]. Some belief air travel as a risk, while few seem to worry about the safety aspects of car transport. What is considered a risk in real life is determined at an individual level, but it is also fixed in time and place. Moreover, this does not apply only to individuals but also to society at large (Porter, 1995, see also the quotation at the beginning of the chapter).

People differ not only in their perception of risks but also in the way, they assess them. The institutional, historical and political context and the (domi-nant) ideology are all important factors in this process (Douglas and Wil-davsky, 1982). For a long time, the debate was dominated by two diametrically opposed approaches: the quantification of objectively observable, calculable risks as opposed to the quantification/description of subjectively perceived potential risks. Both approaches gained followers in the course of time; it comes as no surprise that the first theory is favoured and applied in technol-ogy and economics, while the second has been embraced by the other social sciences. The intrinsic difference would be irrelevant if the outcomes were more or less the same; but research has shown time and again that this is not the case. What emerges is something of a psychometric paradigm: "... *per-ceived risk ... can be distorted by numerous factors, including faulty memory, strong prior beliefs, inability to think probabilistically, and the manner in which risk infor-mation is expressed and communicated to the public*" (Jasanoff, 1998, p. 92).

---

10 However, people and society differ even on this subject: while Sweden was abandoning its nuclear plants, pay-ing investors billions in compensation, Finland decided to invest billions in building new plants. Both decisions were based on the same information/knowledge, but apparently, with different assessments.

Table 2.1 Three different models of risk perception

Model	Epistemology	Source of authority	Policy prescription	
			Style	Mechanism
Realist	Realist	Expert communities	Managerial	Expert advice
Constructivist	Constructivist	Social/interest groups	Pluralist	Public participation
Discursive	Constructivist	Professional discourses	Critical	Social movement

Source: Jasanoff (1998)

As is often the case, thesis and antithesis are followed by synthesis; this time, in the form of the discursive approach (Jasanoff, 1998), which attempts to find a way of uniting the two polar models. Table 2.1 shows the main characteristics of these models.

I shall now take a closer look at these stereotypes.

In what Jasanoff calls the realist approach, everything turns on *"identification of risk, mapping their causal factors, building predictive models of risk relations"* (between cause and effect) and *"expert scientific measurement and calculation..."* (Lupton, 1999, p. 2) – in a nutshell, on measurement and risk determination. This approach implicitly assumes that all risks are quantifiable and that rational decision-makers decide accordingly. Obviously, an objective quantification of a risk is not always straightforward or easy or beyond subjectivity (Croft, 2001). It assumes that experts are the only objective source of knowledge when it comes to risks and implies that what they cannot identify as risks must not be seen as such – at least not at present. It also distinguishes clearly between risk assessment (the measurement of risks) and risk policy, which is seen as communication efforts by the government to convince individuals of the true nature of risks.

In this study, I follow a realist approach to risk. The ultimate goal here is, of course, to deduce risk and risk attitudes from the actual behaviour of households, i.e. the mortgage choices by owner-occupiers.

The second approach – the constructivist approach – is based on what individuals define or experience as a risk. It is culturally determined and heavily dependent on place and time. Risk awareness and risk estimation and assessment are not a constant but *"... can be changed, magnified ... or minimised within knowledge, and to that extent they are particularly up to social definition and construction"* (Adams, 1995, p. 181). Finally, a whole set of psychological factors at individual level determines how a household perceives potential risks and whether it can adequately assess the personal consequences. Society reaches agreement on risks and on how to cope with them individually and collectively by means of broad participation by all the stakeholders.

The third and most recent approach – the discursive approach – tries to 'bridge' the gap between the two former models. Central to this approach is the role of discourse in embedding the meaning of risk in society. Discourse is mobilised within a context of institutional arrangements; but at the same time, they help to structure and restructure it by creating particular understandings of meaning. Alternatively, in the best Foucaultian traditions this process on deciding what the risks are, is merely *"one of the heterogeneous governmental strategies of disciplinary power by which populations and individuals are monitored and managed so as to best meet the goals of democratic humanism"* (Lupton, 1999).

Such a discourse, however, is not necessarily as negative – use or misuse by governments or other stakeholders – as the adherents of the discursive approach believe. It is no longer realistic in our complex modern society to expect each individual to have adequate knowledge of every kind of risk – all the way from nuclear energy to insurance decisions – let alone how to address to them. Quantification by experts may prove useful here; not in a normative manner as the followers of Foucault expect, but in a more prescriptive way, where quantification is seen as a palette of options for decision-makers, showing the implications for individuals and society – in other words, as advice.

Definition of risk attitudes

Risks cannot be assessed in a vacuum; one does not run a risk unless it is counterbalanced by something (potentially) positive, such as the prospect of higher returns and/or lower costs. Usually, higher returns and/or lower costs go hand in hand with high(er) risks. *"The option with the optimum mix of costs, benefit, and risk is selected. The risk associated with that option is acceptable. All others are unacceptable"* (Kaplan and Garrick, 1981, p. 24). I.e. risk is never acceptable unconditionally; it becomes acceptable if some benefit can compensate for the risk. Therefore, it is the decision yielding risk, which is acceptable, not the risk itself. The trade-off between risk and benefits differs amongst individuals and, some argue, on a societal level. It follows, that the risk attitude of an individual decision-maker is his preference for a specific option out of a set of alternatives with different risk/benefit tradeoffs (Fischoff *et al.*, 1981).

Rational choice theory[11] states that households, under equal circumstances, will opt for the deal that they perceive as offering the best costs/returns. If there is any uncertainty in this decision – with regard to, for example, the future costs and risks of a mortgage – then there is no clear-cut optimal choice; the optimum shifts and is dependent on the risk attitude of the decision-maker. A rational decision-maker will not *a priori* choose the option with the lowest costs, but will maximise utility: he will try to minimise the costs (or maximise the returns) plus a fraction of the risk (Eftekhari *et al.*, 2000). To measure the risk attitude of owner-occupiers, it is therefore necessary to ascertain how the costs and risks of the actual choice relate to the costs and risks of all the alternatives within a given institutional context, i.e. within a country. Only then is it possible to say whether the actual choice is optimal

---

11 See Coleman (1995) and Hall (1990) for a more detailed explanation of the rational choice theory.

and whether the owner-occupier has selected an option (mortgage) with a high or low risk profile.

In a standard rational choice model, the risk attitude is considered constant – generally assuming a risk-averse or neutral decision-maker. The question then becomes which alternative is best for the individual decision-maker, i.e. the option with minimum costs and risks. In this study, I do not assume a constant risk attitude; on the contrary, the exact assessment of the risk attitude is precisely the issue here, within a country, but the more so between countries. The central issue here is to compare the actual choice in terms of costs and associated risks – not in terms of mortgage take-up – with all alternative options.

Although the rational choice theory is a popular paradigm in economics, it has often been criticised for failing to give a realistic representation of the true world: household decision-making is far more complex than assumed by the theory (see, for instance, the seminal work by Tversky and Kahneman[12]). The dynamics of housing costs and household income makes an optimal mortgage choice a complex process; owner-occupiers need to make a (subjective) estimate of these factors. A host of research studies have demonstrated that they do not always behave equally rationally (see, for example, Shiller, 1998). In short, owner-occupiers cannot always make the correct 'rational' judgment because they lack the information and the capability to properly assess the (potential) consequences of the various alternatives. In addition, most owner-occupiers get very little opportunity to learn from their mortgage choices, as they make them only once or a few times in their life. Reliance on tradition and the opinions of experts, often intermediaries with their own interests to serve, is frequently the chosen way out.

In conclusion, rational choice theory may help to 'rank' the different options open to the owner-occupier. In the process, it will provide a framework for analysing choice behaviour, indicating whether a deviation from an 'optimum' can be qualified as irrational, risk-averse or the like[13].

Mortgage risks

Although homeownership can enhance the security of individual homeowners and society as a whole, it can just as easily lead to insecurity if circumstances are more dejected. Risk-assessment procedures applied by lenders ensure that, in the short term, the debt-service ratio will remain within limits; therefore, arrears are unlikely. As time passes, however, the probabil-

---

12 Their prospect theory, based on (experimental) psychology, shows vast and persistent deviation from rational behaviour (Tversky and Kahneman, 1992).

13 Note that this framework is more frequently applied to the opposite question of higher returns versus lower risks for financial assets; see Markowitz's portfolio analysis (1952), introducing the now familiar mean-variance framework. The only difference is that the picture is canted; the analysis remains essentially the same.

ity of unforeseen developments increases, as does the probability of arrears and eventual repossessions. Fluctuations in house prices can, for example, encumber households with serious negative equity. Economic transformation, especially after the deregulation of the labour market (more part-time and temporary jobs and self-employment), and demographic factors, such as higher rates of household dissolution and household instability, can spell insecurity for homeowners (and potential homeowners). These adverse events may lead to – as it is often called in the literature – to unsustainable home-ownership. This can be described as a process in which the monthly housing costs become increasingly burdensome for the borrower to bear. In the first stage, household experiences the housing costs as a strain. Then when financial problems endure, they might fall into arrears and finally, they may face repossession (see for instance Maclennan *et al.*, 1997; Ford and Burrows, 1999). Although, frequently used, this concept is rather ill defined; referring to, for instance, the social problems of mortgage arrears or to (financial) difficulties stemming from high housing costs for low income households. In this thesis, I used the concept of unsustainable homeownership simply to refer to the financial commitments households had accepted when taking out a mortgage but which became unsustainable due to changing conditions underpinning the initial financial commitments. In Figure 2.1, this process is depicted.

The crucial factor in this process is the debt-service ratio, i.e. the mortgage costs to household income ratio. If an (unforeseen) adverse event drives up this ratio, the financial commitment may be unsustainable in the end, leading ultimately to arrears and repossession. In this study, I shall focus especially on the mortgage risks for individual homeowners. Give the ambition in this thesis to measure the risks attitudes of owner-occupiers, the emphasis lies naturally on the objectively observable mortgage risk: i.e. mortgage arrears (default risk) and the repossession risk (and negative equity)[14],[15]. In general, default risk can be defined as *the probability and impact (consequences) of a household's inability to continue to meet the financial obligations that it assumed when he bought the property.* This scenario may be brought about by an increase in the housing costs due to e.g. a higher interest rate or a drop in income (in connection with, say, unemployment or divorce). However, not every change in the housing costs or the income automatically leads to a default risk. Many owner-occupiers have some sort of buffer to absorb any unexpected setbacks, especially if their income has risen in relation to their mortgage burden. Therefore, it is not a rise in the housing costs, as such, that matters but a rise

---

14 14, In the literature, many synonyms are used for these types of risks: for instance, mortgage arrears, liquidity, default or credit risk and (early) prepayment, value, residual debt or equity risks.

15 <noot>15 Of course, other types of risks are noticeable as well, e.g. maintenance risks or the social costs of being repossessed. However, these risks do not come autonomous.

Figure 2.1 Trigger events and mortgage risks

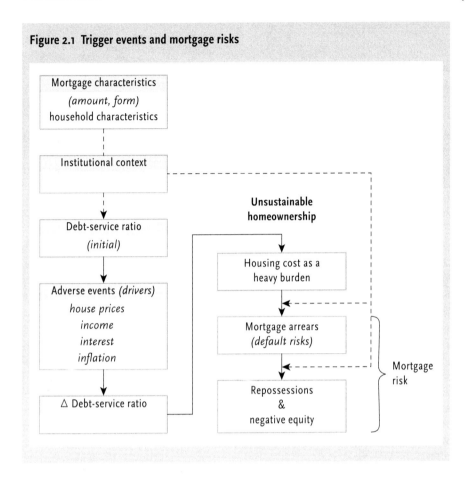

above a certain hurdle level.

Of the second type of mortgage risk, repossession refers to *the probabili-ty that arrears are long lasting and homeownership becomes unsustainable* while negative equity relegate to *the impact (consequences) that the market value of the property is lower than the outstanding mortgage in a situation when the owner-occu-pier is being repossessed.* Developments in house prices are the greatest source of uncertainty for owner-occupiers when it comes to the capital that is 'tied up' in the house. In contrast with the default-risk situation, owner-occupiers can avoid negative equity risks by postponing the sale of the property (the likelihood depends, of course, on the prime reason for selling the house). In such cases, the negative equity is more 'virtual' than actual. Negative equity constitutes a genuine mortgage risk only if it coincides after a period of mort-gage arrears leading to repossession; in this study, I focus solely on this com-bination of events.

Finally, it is important to note that mortgage risks for individual house-holds are also strongly determined by time and place. An unforeseen sharp rise in the debt-service ratio can plunge households straight into problems whereas a gradual rise gives them time to find a solution within their budg-et or to move to a new home. That said, people who have been in debt for a while tend to slip gradually into payment problems (though the actual mo-ment of truth can sometimes be delayed for years). The step from mortgage arrears to repossession is certainly influenced by the institutional context: if the results of payment difficulties are serious and immediate, households will go to great lengths to avoid problems with the lender; in other cases payment difficulties develop more slowly and can last longer.

2.3 Drivers of arrears

What are the drivers of mortgage arrears[16]? The literature offers two main theories to explain the frequency of arrears: the ability-to-pay theory and the equity theory of default. The first is based on the premise that *"mortgagers refrain from loan default as long as income flows are sufficient to meet the periodic payment without undue financial burden"* (Jackson and Kasterman, 1980; Wong et al., 2004). In other words, people do not end up in arrears voluntarily; when the housing costs are not in balance with the monthly income, households are 'forced' into arrears. The crucial factor here is the debt-service ratio: the net mortgage payments divided by net household income. If this ratio rises above a certain level, many individual households will face unsustainable homeownership (starting with experiencing housing costs as a heavy burden), which will increase the probability of arrears and eventually lead to repossession.

The alternative theory states that *"borrowers base their default decision on a rational comparison of the financial costs and returns involved in continuing or terminating mortgage payments"* (ibid.). This means that owner-occupiers stop their mortgage payments if the actual value of their property falls below the outstanding mortgage. The decisive factor in this scenario is not the debt-service ratio but the net equity embedded in the property. In contrast with the US, this approach is, however, not very useful in Europe (Muellbauer, 1997; Böheim and Taylor, 2000), mainly because it implies that the borrower's liability ends when he hands over the title deeds to the lender. In Europe[17], however, borrowers remain liable for any remaining debt, though in most countries this is normally discharged after a few years (in most cases, personal bankruptcy laws restrict the term to 1-3 years). Given that households in the US do not usually go for the prepayment option either, even though this is, theoretically, the most rational course of action[18] and given that, in Europe, the remaining

---

16 Since the overwhelming majority of studies on 'unsustainable homeownership' are concerned with mortgage arrears, this necessarily implies that the literature review is restricted to that aspect (in Chapter 3 I provide information on the other aspects).

17 In the US, no right of recourse exists for lenders, i.e. if the collateral is short on the outstanding debt; the losses are for the lender.

18 Amongst other things, social costs and the credit constraints imposed on a borrower with a bad credit history prompt households to keep paying their debt.

debt is discharged after several years, there is not much difference in actual behaviour of households on either side of the Atlantic.

In the rest of this section, because of its relevancy in a European context, I shall concentrate on the origins of the insecurity that follows from the inability-to-pay hypothesis.

The causes of unsustainable homeownership have been researched extensively, especially in relation to arrears. There has been an interest in the causes and consequences in Anglo-Saxon countries for a long time, but the growth in homeownership and the outstanding mortgage debt in continental Europe have sparked interest elsewhere as well. Most of the studies concentrate on developments in a specific country. I shall pause here to briefly review the literature on countries inside Europe.

It should be noted that the primary concern of this research is on the causes – the drivers – of mortgage arrears. Numerous studies have appeared which attempt to identify the characteristics of households in arrears, some even speculate on how they got there in the first place. These will be briefly addressed in the next chapter. Neither does this study attempt to explain the overall level of mortgage arrears over time or across countries. Variations over time are addressed, for instance, by Brookes et al. (1994) and more recently by Whitley et al. (2005) and Figuera et al. (2005); while the issue of cross-country variation is explained by Doling and Horsewood (2004) and Diaz-Serrano (2005). These studies identify income and income volatility as, by far, the most important variables in arrears over time (business cycle) and between countries.

As mentioned, the UK has a long tradition of research on the extent, causes and effects of unsustainable homeownership. Ford et al. (2002) conclude that unsustainable homeownership in the UK is no longer a problem that arises only in times of economic hardship; in fact, it is becoming more and more of a 'fixture': "... the current incidence of unsustainable homeownership is not 'pathological' or short-lived but rather has become 'normal' and enduring" (p. 170). They offer four arguments to support this opinion:

- the expansion of homeownership, especially among low-income groups;
- demographic transformations, i.e. higher rates of household dissolution and instability;
- economic transformations, particularly the deregulation of the labour market with more part-time and temporary work and self-employment;
- last but not least, the restructuring of the safety-net provisions, notably the restriction of income support for mortgage interest and the introduction of the private sector counterpart: mortgage payment protection insurance.

The authors conclude on the basis of an analysis of the English Housing Survey 1995-1999 that roughly 60% of all payment problems are caused by loss of income (due to e.g. redundancy on the labour market) and 30% by household changes (e.g. divorce). Only 10% are attributable to higher mortgage payments (due to higher interest rates). Kempson et al. (2004) reach similar conclusions, adding that many households tend to pin the blame for their payment problems on external factors. In many studies the scores are low for 'over-commitment' and 'overlooked or withheld' (in the Kempson-study 9% and 11% respectively), even though many budget studies have shown that quite a lot of people end up in difficulties because of poor financial planning. Often, mortgage arrears are not the only debts; many people are behind with payments for other obligations as well (e.g. energy bills).

Both studies point out that households do not always fall into arrears for one reason alone; usually, as time progresses, arrears develop through a combination of factors. The CML (2005), quoting the Citizens Advice Bureaux, states that 60% of all households in arrears felt that their debt was caused by multiple factors. These combinations of factors and the different time schedules that accompany them create serious problems in any (quantitative) analysis.

Böheim and Taylor (2000) were the first to use panel data, i.e. the British Household Panel Survey, to explain arrears and repossessions (both in the rental and homeownership sector). The causes they identify are more or less the same as those identified in the studies discussed above, but they also highlight the role of personal factors (money mismanagement) and expectations. They draw attention to the fact that some households are permanently short of money, thereby concluding that financial problems in the past are the best indicator for financial problems in the future[19]; 60% of all households in arrears managed to escape their financial problems within the year, but only temporarily. Böheim and Taylor constructed an indicator for financial shocks, using both the expectations of individual households and actual developments; financial shocks emerged as a key route to unsustainable homeownership (more than income loss, taken on its own).

In other countries, research on the extent, causes and effects of unsustainable homeownership is still in its infancy. Recent studies revealed that in France, Germany and the Netherlands, the main reasons for arrears are loss of income following unemployment and divorce (Bosvieux and Vorms, 2003; Kloth, 2004; Elsinga and Dol, 2003); an unanticipated increase of housing costs nor money management problems seems to be a major cause in these countries.

Interestingly, hardly any research of this type has been carried out in countries with relatively high levels of arrears (e.g. Italy, Belgium).

---

19 This is why, in any risk assessment procedure by lenders, past credit history plays the most important role, more than actual loan-to-income or loan-to-value ratios; these can be and are raised when necessary.

Table 2.2 Causes of arrears (selected countries, in %)

	(1)	(2)	(3)	(4)	(5)	(6)	(7)
Belgium	13.6	9.3	3.9	0.6	55.4	4.8	12.4
Denmark	17.8	10.9	13.2	2.6	38.2	1.6	15.7
France	15.9	9.1	7.8	2.8	56.2	2.9	5.3
Netherlands	14.7	22.4	3.5	2.2	42.0	9.8	5.3
UK	19.2	20.3	2.6	2.6	33.4	7.9	14.0

Source: Neuteboom and Dol (2005)

Columns (1) Work > benefit, (2) Higher housing costs, (3) Moving from rented sector, (4) Moving within owner-occupied sector, (5) Drop in income, (6) Family > single (parent), (7) Personal factors (money mismanagement, attitudes); the differences in the actual level of arrears is quite high, ranging from below 1% in Denmark, the Netherlands and the UK to nearly 5% in Belgium (see Figure 1.1).

A new approach was adopted by Neuteboom and Dol (2005), who re-searched the causes of mortgage arrears by applying a duration analysis on longitudinal panel data (ECHP) from eight European countries over the period 1994-2001. Neuteboom and Dol studied individual changes in income, housing costs etcetera and looked at whether these caused any future financial difficulties or arrears. The main results are set out in Table 2.2. The percentages in Table 2.2 identified changes that took place at household level prior to the arrears.

As shown in Table 2.2, the main underlying reason is a fall in income and/or a rise in housing costs (not due to moving house), followed by a change in socio-economic position (loss of job) and personal factors (payment discipline, attitude, etc.). Mobility between the rental and the homeownership sector plays a somewhat insignificant role in most countries. Finally, it appears that, in some countries, personal factors (money mismanagement, attitudes) are an important cause of arrears as well (Denmark and the UK), while in others (France and the Netherlands) paying discipline and attitude seem to be stricter. It should also be remembered that in 1994-2001 many countries in Europe were experiencing an economic boom, implying not only rather low levels of arrears but also lower probabilities of drops in income and rising interest rates.

In conclusion, it seems that a complex mix of socio-economic and personal circumstances causes mortgage arrears. It has been suggested that three, possibly interrelated, sets of factors are at work here (Ford et al., 2002). The first concerns macro factors, such as interest rates, changes in government subsidies and social security systems. The maximum loan-to-income or loan-to-value ratio also has a profound effect on risk. These factors are largely responsible for developments through time or between countries, i.e. the overall levels of default. What they do not explain is the variation in the incidence of arrears between individuals. The second set concerns income and expenditure on a household level. Fluctuations in household income because of job loss or short-term work can lead to serious payment problems. A decline in the second income, if one of the partners starts to work fewer hours (for whatever reason), could also have repercussions, as mortgage obligations are being increasingly based on double earnings. Long-term illness and divorce also belong in the second set. Unanticipated costs, such as a rise in mortgage interest rates, can also increase the payment burden. Finally, the third set is more personal: people may have budgeting problems or specific attitudes, or they may set quite different spending priorities.

2.4 Modelling mortgage risks

Section 2.2 defined the concepts of 'risk' and 'risk attitude'. The previous section reviewed the potential sources of these risks (in terms of Section 2.2, *hazards*). This section will combine them in one conceptual model, which will be interpreted in more econometric terms in Chapters 4 and 5 and will serve as the basis for answering the principal aim of this study, i.c. estimating the risk attitudes of borrowers.

To ascertain the risk – in this case the mortgage risk – we need answers to three questions (Kaplan and Garrick, 1981):

- Which events (hazards) can have (potentially) negative consequences for individual homeowners?
- What is the probability of such an event taking place? And finally,
- What are the exact consequences?

In other words, risks are combinations of hazards, probabilities and impact (consequences) for individual owner-occupiers. Kaplan and Garrick (1981) present this as a triplet:

$$R = \{<s, p_s, x_s>\}$$
$$s = 1..S$$

In which $s = 1..S$ is the risk source, p_s is the probability of an unexpected, unwelcome situation and x_s is the impact, i.e. the negative financial consequences.

This concept of quantification of risk as represented by Kaplan and Garrick's triplet can be illustrated by a simple example of measuring the affordability of homeownership (see Box 2.1). How can this concept be used to measure mortgage risks? The answers to the above questions provide the guidelines.

- *Which event (hazards) can have (potentially) negative consequences for individual homeowners?* Section 2.2 identified the hazards ($s = 1..S$) for the individual owner-occupier: amongst others, a change in household income, interest rates, inflation, and/or house prices.
- *What is the probability of such an event taking place?* If we assume that the

Box 2.1 Measuring the affordability of homeownership

Suppose we are interested in the affordability of homeownership. Let us assume that affordability is merely a function of interest rates, household income and outstanding mortgage debt. Hence:

$$Aff_t = Aff_t(r_t, Y_t, M_{t-1})$$

Since interest rates are notoriously uncertain, so is affordability. It is easy to conceive a scenario in which interest rates rise, thereby pushing up housing costs and lowering affordability ($\Delta r_t \succ 0 \Rightarrow \Delta Aff_t \prec 0$). So, it is easy to use the model to compute the consequences in terms of housing costs and affordability for a whole range of interest rates. In Kaplan and Garrick's triplet representation, we already have the different scenarios s and the consequences x_s; all that is needed is an estimation of p_s, the probability of a specific scenario. Of course, no one can say what lies ahead, but we can use historical data on the interest rate distribution as the closest proximity to any such an event happening in the future, i.e. p_s^*. The historical distribution of the interest rates is shown in the figure below left; the corresponding consequences are shown in the figure below right.

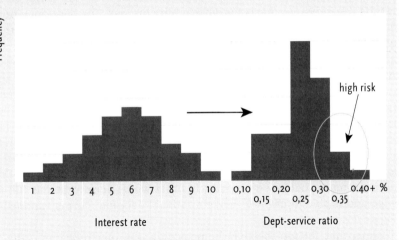

Interest rate   Dept-service ratio

This is a simple, stylised example with just one independent variable (r_t); in theory, it can easily be extended with numerous other variables. All that is needed is the definition of a series of scenario s i.e. a combination of expected developments in the various relevant factors, an assessment of the possible consequences x_s when scenario s occurs and knowledge of the (joint) probability distribution of the different scenarios p_t.

---

* Note, that if, for whatever reasons, some sort of structural break has occurred (or is to be expected), the historical distribution is not always the right choice; one should calibrate accordingly.

above hazards are historically determined and path-dependent, we can use their historical probability distributions to estimate possible future developments (p_s).

- *What are the exact consequences?* There are two crucial factors in this analysis. Firstly, the expected costs under different conditions. Secondly, the debt-service ratio; if this ratio exceeds a certain level (hurdle rate), the result will eventually be arrears and/or repossession[20] (x_s). It is ultimately the combination of both that shapes consumer behaviour.

The above answers were used to design a model for measuring mortgage costs and risks. That model simulates scenarios of the underlying variables, namely: interest rates, house prices, household income, etc., over the relevant time horizon. Secondly, it computes (the discounted value of) the annual net mortgage costs and debt-service ratio[21]. The annual net costs and the debt-service ratio are then no longer characterised by one – i.e. the most likely – outcome, but by a probability distribution of all possible outcomes. The mean can serve as an indication of the expected costs, while the variation in the results can serve as a basis for determining the risk. The development of the debt-service ratio over time can serve as a 'trigger' for the mortgage risks (arrears and repossession).

It was mentioned in the introduction that any comparison of the costs and risks of mortgages should take account of the differences between the institutional contexts, the characteristics of individual owner-occupiers, and the fact that the mortgage markets are still national markets. Therefore, besides scenarios on future income, interest etcetera attention needs to be paid to institutions, household characteristics and supply (limitations). The decision-maker, the borrower, has to decide which product delivers the lowest costs and risks over the full mortgage period in his own case. It is assumed that the decision-maker behaves rationally; in other words, ideally, he has full knowledge and is able to use it to make a rational decision. This is summed up in Figure 2.2.

Note, that for (prospective) homeowners, the macro-factors – the uncertainty about future developments – are more or less equal, but the consequences may be different; for example, a change in interest rates will affect all homeowners, but to a different extent depending on the outstanding debt and the mortgage type. Life cycle and income changes are, in principal, based on the individual characteristics of a household, namely: income, education, and household type (size), etc.

In short, the decision-making process is influenced by a set of macro-variables and micro-variables; the actual choice depends on the homeowner's assessment of the costs and risks of the alternatives available to him.

Finally, how does this conceptual model fit in with the general aim of this study to capture the differences in risk attitudes – if any – between countries?

---

20 Obviously, the pace at which all of this leads to payment difficulties is dependent on the context.
21 I.e. linking expected housing costs with net household income.

Figure 2.2 Conceptual model

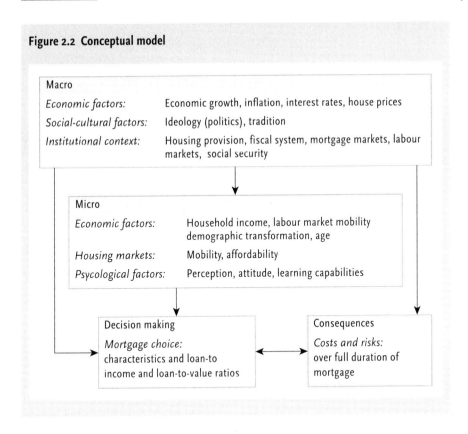

As explained earlier, analysing the actual choice that households make with all other options ranked in order of risks will suffice. All the options should be framed in terms of costs and risk, corrected for differences in institutions, household characteristics and the supply side (restrictions). Therefore, the conceptual model to calculate the net costs and risks of a mortgage (depicted in Figure 2.2) can readily be applied.

3 Mortgage markets and mortgage take-up in Europe[22]

3.1 Introduction

In Chapter 1 it was suggested – and to some extent demonstrated – that mortgage take-up across Europe varies widely at both micro and macro level. In other words, there are differences in the degree to which, and the way in which, individual households in the various countries use a mortgage to finance homeownership. It was also argued that a simple output indicator such as mortgage take-up says little about the actual risks facing owner-occupiers; primarily because national differences in the institutional context, the characteristics of owner-occupiers and the national mortgage market are left out in such comparison; issues that are assumed to be of importance.

In this chapter, these assumptions are explored more deeply. After discussing mortgage take-up at micro and macro level (Section 3.2), I shall present the institutional differences across Europe with the aid of a financial regime index (Section 3.3) and then discuss the characteristics of owner-occupiers (Section 3.4) and structure of national mortgage markets (Section 3.5). The primary aim of this chapter is to provide some basic information that can offer further insight into the similarities and differences in mortgage take-up and institutions and provide ample proof of the above assumptions. Second, it will assist in the interpretation of the empirical results in Chapters 5 and 6.

Interested readers will find an abundance of more detailed analyses on housing and finance markets in the literature; see, for instance: ECB (2003); Mercer Oliver Wyman (2003, 2005); consecutive studies of the European Mortgage Federation (2003a, 2005); Donner (2000) and Neuteboom (2002, 2004). For a more detailed analysis of the differences and similarities between demographic trends, labour markets and social security systems, see Horsewood and Neuteboom (2006).

In this thesis, primarily six countries are analysed and compared: Belgium, Denmark, France, Italy, the Netherlands and the UK; hereafter referred to as EU6. These countries were chosen partly on pragmatic grounds; the availability of relevant data played a particularly important role. At the same time, they reflect more or less the current differences in mortgage take-up by owner-occupiers within Europe. For example, though Belgium and the Netherlands share many institutions, the mortgage take-up is, in fact, extremely divergent. Conversely, the Netherlands and the UK have a more or less identical mortgage take-up, but different (social) institutions.

Secondly, the reference year for this study is 2003, the latest year for which sufficient information was available. Notwithstanding long-term EU coopera-

---

22 In this chapter, occasionally, a reference is made to Europe; this refers to the 15 EU member states, before the enlargement of 2005.

Table 3.1 Key characteristics of the six countries in the study (EU6, 2003)

	Belgium	Denmark	France	Italy	Netherlands	UK
Demography						
Population (*ml.*)	10.2	5.3	59.6	57.8	16.1	59.2
Households (*ml.*)	4.3	2.4	24.5	22.0	6.9	24.1
Annual growth of number of households (%)	0.8	0.9	1.2	n.a.	1.6	1.0
Dependency ratio[1] (%)	52	50	53	48	47	53
Share 65+ (%)	17.0	14.8	16.3	18.4	13.7	15.7
Economy						
GDP (*EU 15 = 100*)	117.7	121.6	112.3	107.2	125.5	116.2
Annual economic growth (%)	1.5	0.5	1.2	0.4	0.1	2.0
Inflation (%)	1.6	2.4	1.9	2.6	3.9	1.3
Interest rate[2] (%)	4.2	4.3	4.1	4.3	4.1	4.6
Activity rate[3] (%)	59.6	75.1	63.3	56.1	73.6	71.5
Unemployment (%)	8.0	5.6	9.5	8.4	3.7	4.9
Social security *Unemployment*						
Minimum duration (year)	Unlimit.	8½	3	½	½	½
Replacement rate[4] (%)	65.9	81.8	67.7	71.0	86.2	45.0
Pension						
Retirement age (year)	58.5	60.9	58.8	59.9	62.2	62.3
Replacement rate[5] (%)	82.2	41.9	59.1	69.5	53.2	33.6
Housing market						
Homeownership rate (%)	68	52	56	77	52	69
Growth (*in %p*)[6]	9	-1	9	16	10	11
House prices[7] (*annual change in %*)	1.6	1.1	1.4	2.3	2.8	3.4

Source: Eurostat, European Community Household Panel, European Central Bank, Housing Statistics in the European Union, Bank of International Settlements; Scruggs and Allan (2003)

1. Dependency ratio is the number of household dependants younger than 15 and older than 65 divided by the total population number of households aged 15 to 64; 2. 10-year Government bonds; 3. Percentage of persons employed for more than 12 hours a week; 4. Benefits as a percentage of previous earnings from paid employment (net); 5. State pensions only; 6. Percentage point, over the period 1980-2003; 7. Average over 1970-2003 in real terms.

tion, it is important to point out that differences exist not only in institutions but in economic cycles as well. Consequently, this section will finish off with a brief profile of the six countries in this study as in 2003 (see Table 3.1).

Across Europe, demographic patterns are dominated by two trends: individualisation and ageing, both of which van be observed in many European countries, albeit to varying degrees. The trend towards individualisation is reflected in the rise in the number of single parents and single-person households (also due to some extent to the ageing population) and implies less stability in both household size and income. The influence of individualisation in household composition is reverberating on the risks of homeownership. To begin with, robust growth in the number of single households is increasing the demand for (owner-occupier) housing, which, in turn, co-determines price trends in the owner-occupier market. Meanwhile, uncertainty about the stability of the family is adding to the sense of insecurity; household dissolution as a percentage of the total number of families ranges annually from 0.5% in Portugal to 2.9% in the Netherlands; the household dissolution rate in other countries lies somewhere between these two extremes.

As mortgage payments are generally based on expectations of the future income streams of the household, the frequency, nature and consequences of interruptions in household income are crucially important. Two factors play a particularly important role here: the stability of the household as such (see before) and fluctuations in household income because of economic changes at macro level (linked to economic growth) and micro level. The workings of the labour market and the social security system are critical, and increasing European cooperation and globalisation heavily influence both.

Since the early post-war years, there has been a shift away from permanent, secure jobs to more atypical or precarious jobs: more self-employment, part-time jobs, fixed-term and casual jobs and more frequent periods of unemployment. This process has been accelerated in recent years by the trend towards more flexible labour markets. Note as well that the differences in unemployment rates across Europe reflect different economic cycles.

These trends also have major implications for the social security systems in Europe. A high level of social security is counterbalanced by huge government spending and high taxes (making labour more expensive). In periods of economic decline, as witnessed by many countries in the 1980s and early 1990s, social security systems came under severe pressure. During these years, national governments across Europe tackled the high unemployment rates primarily by cutting labour costs (taxes) and stimulating employment. The downside of this strategy was, of course, growing budget deficits that, in turn, were addressed by cuts in government spending; hence, it was inevitable that the social system would be restructured. This trend was visible in most countries in Europe, with Scandinavian countries, the Netherlands and the UK as the frontrunners. France and Germany were far slower to proceed down this road (Horsewood and Neuteboom, 2006).

3.2 Mortgage take-up across Europe

A macro approach: outstanding mortgages (see Table 3.2)
In most EU countries, the majority of households live in owner-occupied dwellings (Table 3.1). Although there is a high incidence of outright ownership in the EU, many households need a mortgage to buy a home. Personal savings and family loans used to be important factors but are now declining across Europe. In addition, more and more people are remortgaging to release housing equity. These trends have led to a high level of outstanding mortgage debt throughout Europe. Indeed, in the 1990s, the outstanding mortgage debt in Europe more or less trebled. In 2003, outstanding mortgage debt add up to €3.9 trillion[23] and is equal to one third of the entire gross domestic product (GDP) in the European Union (EU 15). Mortgages also account for over 40% of all outstanding bank credit. The growth has been so spectacular that, in many countries, the outstanding mortgage debt has even outstripped national debt. This situation can largely be explained by the deregulation of finance markets, strong economic growth, the increase in homeownership and a steep house price rise in real terms.

Despite closer European cooperation, there is no uniform pattern of mortgage take-up; at present, the level and growth rate differ considerably from country to country. In absolute terms, the UK and Germany do have the largest national mortgage markets, but in terms of GDP, the Netherlands and (at a push) Denmark have the largest outstanding mortgage debt. This has not always been the case; the latter two countries in particular have experienced a sharp rise in outstanding mortgage debt in the past few decades. At the end of the 1980s they were both somewhere in the middle (Van Rooij and Stokman, 1999); things (appear to) have moved rapidly since then.

However, the outstanding mortgage debt expressed in percentage of GDP is a rather poor indicator of the risks of a high debt position. After all, it says very little about the total payment capability of the individual households, which are responsible for this debt. If it is spread across many households and the size of the individual debt is matched against the ability to pay, then not much can go wrong. But this situation may change if the mortgage debt is disproportionately spread across different (categories of) households; this creates risks for individual households with a large debt and eventually for the financial sector as a whole. One indicator of an unequal spread is the share of the outstanding mortgage debt borne by households with a high debt-service ratio; 30 to 35% is generally regarded as risky.

Table 3.2 clearly shows that in both the Netherlands and Denmark – which have the highest outstanding mortgage debt in percentage of GDP – only a

---

23 The growth in outstanding mortgage debt continues, in 2005 it has risen to €5.1 trillion.

Table 3.2 Outstanding mortgages (EU6, 2003)

	Outstanding mortgage debt			Idem, in the hands of high risk-groups*		
	Absolute in billions	Absolute in % GDP	Cumulative growth**	Share DSR > 30%	Share DSR > 35%	Share DSR in % GDP
Belgium	78.3	28.5	8.2	2.8	2.1	0.2
Denmark	165.9	87.5	27.1***	1.6	0.8	0.7
France	533.9	24.7	0.9	9.0	3.9	1.3
Italy	184.3	13.8	8.8	25.2	16.2	1.2
Netherlands	476.5	99.9	49.7	3.2	2.0	1.2
UK	1,129.6	70.4	15.9	13.2	8.5	3.3

Source: Eurostat, European Community Household Panel, European Central Bank, Housing Statistics in the European Union, Brounen et al. (2005)

* Here, high risk groups are defined as households with a high debt-service ratio (DSR); ** Over the period 1991-2003; *** 1993.

small part of this debt lies with households in the high-risk group. Conversely, in the country with the lowest outstanding mortgage debt, Italy, as much as 25% is borne by high-risk groups. The only 'blot on the landscape' is the UK, which combines a high outstanding debt with a relatively high share in the hands of high-risk groups.

Overall, there are wide differences in mortgage take-up in absolute terms and in relation to GDP, but if we focus on the share borne by the high-risk groups, the ranking changes dramatically and the differences turn out to be smaller.

A view from the micro level (see Tables 3.3 and 3.4)

Mortgage take-up also differs at micro level. In the comparison that follows the focus is on recent buyers, i.e. homeowners who bought their present property less than two years ago. These households provide a more up-to-date, and hence, a more apt picture of the preferences and choices in the various countries.

There are three indicators on a micro level that provide further insight into mortgage take-up: loan-to-income (LTI), loan-to-value (LTV), and debt-service ratio (DSR). The average outstanding mortgage debt as such says very little about the risks and the risk attitude of individual owner-occupiers. The outstanding mortgage debt in relation to the value of the property and/or the net household income is a better indicator; a high loan-to-value ratio would constitute a potential capital risk for the individual owner-occupier (and the lender) if a crisis were to strike the property market. A high loan-to-income ratio potentially increases the probability of payment difficulties if the household suddenly suffers a drop in income.

Not surprisingly, under these conditions, loan-to-value ratios differ considerably across Europe (Neuteboom, 2002), ranging from – on average – 80% or more in Northwest Europe to less than 50% in Southern Europe. For first-time buyers it can be as high as 112% in some countries, (e.g. the Netherlands). Traditionally, households can opt for three sources of finance: mortgage lending,

Table 3.3 Mortgage take-up in the EU6: a micro view (2003)

	Belgium	Denmark	France	Italy	Netherlands	UK
Non-movers						
Debt	€ 53,914	€ 136,776	€ 84,812	€ 55,317	€ 119,695	€ 91,777
Loan to value	0.52	0.61	0.65	0.47	0.58	0.62
Loan to income	1.36	3.19	2.24	1.82	3.57	2.05
Dept-service ratio	0.10	0.12	0.16	0.18	0.12	0.16
Recent buyers						
Debt	€ 69,291	€ 182,937	€ 104,439	€ 65,352	€ 194,982	€ 123,642
Loan to value	0.67	0.82	0.79	0.56	0.95	0.84
Loan to income	1.66	4.76	3.07	2.29	6.26	2.72
Dept-service ratio	0.13	0.16	0.24	0.22	0.21	0.23
First-time buyers						
Debt	€ 74,023	€ 193,336	€ 105,059	€ 58,586	€ 191,372	€ 118,741
Loan to value	0.71	0.86	0.80	0.50	0.93	0.80
Loan to income	1.95	5.16	3.10	1.56	6.07	3.29
Dept-service ratio	0.14	0.17	0.24	0.19	0.23	0.22

Source: Eurostat, European Community Household Panel, European Central Bank; European Mortgage Federation

Average by country, LTV is based on outstanding debt and self-reported house price; LTI based on *net* household income.

personal savings and family loans. Households in Denmark, the Netherlands and the UK tend to choose mortgage lending, in France (and Germany) people are more inclined towards savings, while in Southern Europe the emphasis lies on a combination of savings and family loans.

Loan-to-income ratios range from just over 6 for recent buyers with a mortgage in the Netherlands to less than 2 in Belgium and Italy. Note that the definition of the loan-to-income ratio used here is based on the net household income instead of some definition of gross income, which may be more widely used but still makes for misleading comparisons, certainly in a cross-country framework.

The debt-service ratio forms the third and crucial element in the analysis and estimation of both risks and risk attitudes (see Chapter 2). This indicator sheds some light on the net cost of the mortgage chosen by an owner-occupier (see Table 3.4 below), taking account of both the national systems of housing provision and the individual characteristics of the homeowner. At the same time, the debt-service ratio could serve as a prime indicator of unsustainable homeownership: a high debt-service ratio triggers arrears, etc. Note that the debt-service ratio for recent buyers is high in both France and Italy, in contrast with the low outstanding mortgage debt in these countries. This somewhat paradoxical situation can be explained by the fact that households in these countries are so preoccupied on repaying the debt as soon as pos-

Table 3.4 Mortgage take-up in the EU6: characteristics of mortgage contracts (2001/2)

| | Type[1] | Duration (years) | Gross interest rate (%)[2] | Fixed interest rate period | | | Early prepayment (penalty) |
				Type[3]	Duration (years)	Share (%)	
Belgium	Repay	20	5.2	Ren, Fix	20	75	Yield maintenance fees
Denmark	Repay	30	4.9	Fix, Ref	30	20	Administrative costs maximised by law to 0.6%
France	Repay	17	4.1	Fix, Ref	12	40	Minimum of 6 months interest or 3% (secured by law)
Italy	Repay	15	4.5	Fix, Ref	1/15	40	Fees are ~2%
Netherlands	Endow	30	4.6	Rev, Fix	11	90	Yield maintenance fees
UK	Endow/Repay	25	6.5	Rev, Ren	< 1	100	Administrative costs < 0.3%

Source: Eurostat, European Community Household Panel, European Central Bank, Housing statistics in the European Union, Mercer Oliver Wyman (2003)

1. Repay(ment): annuity/serial mortgage; Endow(ment): savings or investment mortgage; 2. Gross mortgage interest rate for a standard mortgage with a fixed-interest period of 10 years, 1999; 3. Rev(iewable): the interest rate is changed at the end of the agreed period, the level being fixed by the lender; Ren(egotiable): the interest rate is changed at the end of the agreed period, with the borrower renegotiating the interest rate for the following period; Ref(erenced): the interest rate changes on the basis of an index pre-agreed by the parties, e.g. the interest on a given government bond; Fix(ed): the interest rate is fixed for the full term of the mortgage.

sible (in less than 15 years, see below) that they are prepared to accept a high debt-service ratio for a relatively short period.

Households can choose from literally hundreds of mortgages, each with a different risk profile. Despite the overwhelming choice, there are, in general, very few actual product differences. By far the most popular mortgages across Europe are still the annuity and/or the serial mortgage (see Table 3.4). Indeed, in many countries these are all that are on offer for the general public. Holders of such mortgages make capital as well as interest payments. This is in contrast with endowment and investment mortgages, where the holder does not make any payments towards the principal but deposits sums of money in a savings account so that he can pay off the entire debt when the mortgage expires. The downside of this option is that the mortgage-holder pays interest on the entire sum throughout the full duration of the mortgage contract.

Besides the amortisation scheme, typical duration and fixed interest rate period are important mortgage contract specifications; both are quite divergent between countries. The average duration of a mortgage varies from 10 to 15 years in France and Italy to a standard 30 years in the Netherlands[24].

One of the more conventional ways in which owner-occupiers can reduce payment risks is to take out a mortgage with a long term of fixed interest. In Europe, the options range from one month (or less) to 30 years or more. A

---

24 Nowadays, in Sweden and Japan, it is even possible to take out a mortgage for 40-50 years.

variable interest rate is generally lower than a fixed interest rate, but it can fluctuate widely within the lifetime of the mortgage and affect the monthly payments accordingly. A fixed interest rate offers a large degree of assurance about the monthly costs but, as usual, it comes at a price: higher interest rates (the yield curve is normally upward sloping).

3.3 Institutions that matter

One of main themes in this study is that an output indicator, such as mortgage take-up discussed in the previous section, is not a good indicator of either the costs or risks that homeowners take on neither for the underlying risk attitudes. Institutional differences may go some way in explaining this difference. This section therefore analyses the differences and similarities in the institutional context across Europe.

First, we need to define the concept of institutions and institutional context; both definitions will be used interchangeably in this study. A basic definition of institutions is: *"organisations, or mechanisms of social structure, governing the behaviour of two or more individuals"*.

A clear distinction needs to be drawn here between external and internal institutionalisation (Priemus, 1983). External institutionalisation consists of rules (laws) that are imposed – usually by the government – on the market players. Internal institutions consist of the norms and regulations imposed by private organisations. An intermediate form, in which agreements are reached at sector level on the conduct of companies and organisations, is coming under increasing pressure from financial authorities[25]. Here I shall focus primarily on external institutions. The internal institutions governing the 'mortgage industry' are discussed in Section 3.5.

Here, various factors are relevant. The legal aspects (e.g. consumer protection), the social context (labour market flexibility, social security and financial support), systems of housing provision, and the structure of the property and mortgage markets all play a role. All these factors influence the (net) costs of homeownership and the distribution of risks among the different agents (borrowers, lenders and/or the government). Both the social context and the system of housing provision have a key influence on demand as they broaden the expenditure opportunities of households and reduce uncertainty about future income. This confidence leads to greater risk-taking behaviour – expressed in higher loan-to-value and loan-to-income ratios – as well as a preference for long-term mortgages. Consumer protection and legislation, on the other hand, have a direct impact on the supply side of the market. Strong consumer rights

---

25 Hampering competition and hence not in the interest of consumers.

shift the risks of homeownership from the borrower to the mortgage lender; consumer rights limit the likelihood of arrears, with short-term and low loan-to-value mortgages as a natural reaction from lenders.

The remainder of this section will concentrate on the housing finance system and its context. Labour market issues and social security systems – of prime importance as well – have already been touched on in Section 3.1.

Systems of housing provision (see Table 3.5)
Across Europe there is a wide variety of schemes, which are designed to guarantee the affordability and attainability of homeownership (sometimes only for specific groups) and to limit the accompanying risks. These schemes have been overhauled in most countries in recent decades. Two trends have emerged: a shift from production subsidies to consumption subsidies and a stronger focus on the market (Ball and Grilli, 1997). The previously mentioned financial and economic crisis that hit many countries in the late 1980s is partly responsible for this turn-around. While Southern European countries continued to operate subsidy systems, their Northern neighbours were pushing through fast and radical changes (Donner, 2000). Though it would even be fair to say that, in terms of their impact on housing and mortgage market outcomes, the influence of simple tax deduction systems in Northern countries is much greater than the complex and multiple housing provisions systems in Southern Europe. See Doling and Ford (2003) and Elsinga et al. (2007) for a more up-to-date review of the developments and policy intentions in various European countries.

Mortgage interest tax relief is not only the most visible and direct form of subsidy in most countries, but also the one involving by far the biggest budget. With the exception of France, Germany and the UK, all European countries run some system of mortgage interest tax relief (Boelhouwer et al., 2003). In Italy and Denmark, the rate is proportional; in other countries (Italy), the deductions are maximised (at a level that is mostly irrelevant to the average owner-occupier). In Belgium[26] and the Netherlands, mortgage interest tax relief depends on marginal income rates.

The importance and applicability of other mortgage-subsidy schemes differ considerably according to the country. Usually, there are various co-existent schemes that may accumulate for some households and be denied to others. In general, eligibility depends on income, age, whether purchase or maintenance is involved, and/or the position of the (potential) buyer on the housing market. These schemes can be split roughly into four categories:

---

26 In Belgium mortgage interest tax relief is maximised; on the other hand interest and repayments are both deductible. Recent policy changes in Belgium (2005) have improved the mortgage interest tax relief facility for Belgian homeowners.

Table 3.5 Mortgage interest tax relief and non-fiscal subsidies schemes in selected European countries (EU6, 2001)

	Belgium	Denmark	France	Italy	Netherlands	UK
Mortgage interest tax relief	Yes, marginal rates[1]	Yes, flat rate	No	Yes, flat rate, max.	Yes, marginal	None[2]
Subsidy rate[3]	23.1%	31.0%	--	11.4%	37.2%	--
Non-fiscal (*examples*)	Minor subsidy programme for low income groups	Minor subsidy programme for young and retired	Housing allowance scheme	Minor subsidy programme for low income groups	Minor subsidy programme for low income groups	None
Subsidy rate	0.4%	0.1%	3.7%	0.3%	--	--
Guarantees	Yes, limited	Yes	Yes	No	Yes	No (private)
Saving schemes	No	Yes, limited	Yes	No	No	No
Subsidised loan	Yes	No	Yes	Yes	No	No

Sources: Neuteboom (2000), European Community Household Panel, European Central Bank (2003), Mercer Oliver Wyman (2003), Doling and Ford (2003)

1. Repayments are also deductible; 2. Abolition completed in April 2001; 3. Estimated effective subsidy rate in % of gross mortgage payment.

- subsidised loans: loans which are offered at a lower rate of interest than the commercial rate, e.g. the *Prêt à taux zero* in France;
- interest subsidies: income-dependent interest subsidies (comparable with the housing allowance system in the rental sector), e.g. the *Agevolata* scheme in Italy and *Aide Personnalisé au Logement* in France;
- savings/lending plans, e.g. the famous *Bausparkassen* in Germany and the *Caisse d'Epargne* in France;
- guarantees by public or private institutions: the Netherlands is the only country in Europe with a private guarantee institution, the *Nationale Hypotheek Garantie* (with public backing). Public equivalents exist in, amongst other countries, Denmark and France.

Table 3.5 also shows the average subsidy as a percentage of the gross mortgage payments for the various countries. This percentage is an average of what all borrowers in the respective countries have received (in 2001). The differences speak for themselves and are not surprising given the above facts and the current debates on the issue.

Borrowers' protection
Governments can also exercise a more direct influence on the outcomes of housing and mortgage markets: the legal context defines – or at least adjusts – the distribution of mortgage risks among borrowers, lenders and the government. There are, moreover, differences in the way governments define the rights of borrowers. Some aspects are addressed in Table 3.6 (see EMF, 2003b; Dol and Neuteboom 2005 for a more exhaustive analysis).

One important benchmark is the European code of conduct: an agreement between lenders and the European Commission regarding minimum informa-

Table 3.6 Borrowers' protection (EU6, 2001/3)[1]

	Belgium	Denmark	France	Italy	Netherlands	UK
Pre-contractual rights of borrower						
Code of conduct	+	+	– [1]	+	+	–
Information rights	++	–	++	++	–	+
APRC[2]	+	+	+	+	+	+
Pre-contractual duties of lender						
Responsible lending	+	+	+	–	+	++
Linking of services	Authorised	Not regulated	Forbidden	n.a.	Not regulated	Regulated
Insurances	0.6%	0.6%	0.7%	0.2%	0.4%[3]	0.9%
Conclusion						
Written offer binds	+	+	+	–	+	–
Right of reflection	+	+	++	–	–	+
Closing fees	2.1%	2.1%	2.2%	1.2%	2.2%	0.3%
Early prepayment						
Right of withdrawal	–	–	–	–	–	–
Early prepayment	– –	+	–	–	– –	+
Usury regulation	–	+	+	+	–	–
Arrears						
Contractual penalties	–	–	+	–	–	++
Unpaid interest	+	–	+	–	+	+
Financial support	Yes	No	Yes	No	No[4]	Yes
Repossession						
Juridical system	Notaries	Juridical	Juridical	Juridical	Notaries	Notaries
Repossession time (month)	18	6	15–45	60–84	6	8–12
Administrative costs	18.7%	n.a.	7.0%	n.a.	3.0%	2.6–7.0%
Over-indebtedness	+	–	+	–	+	++

Source: European Mortgage Federation (2003b); OECD (2004)

1. + Indicates compliance with the European code of conduct in national legislation, ++ extra requirements and – restriction and/or not implied; generally a positive sign indicates a favourable context for borrowers 2. APRC = Annual percentage rate of charge, i.e. gross interest rate plus additional costs; 3. Insurance obligation by lender. 4. Specific support not available, but generous social security systems. Note the availability of a large, competitive rental sector as an alternative (Neuteboom and Dol, 2005).

tion and ground rules for borrowers. This agreement has since been embedded in the legislative systems of all EU countries. Some countries, including France and the UK, have added extra requirements, such as a duty of care for lenders, which makes lenders legally accountable for their lending practices, i.e. households in potentially risky situations should not be allowed to take out disproportionate loans.

Further, there are no uniform procedures in Europe for households in payment difficulties or for repossessions. Penalty clauses are banned in many countries while repossession times range from less than six months in the Netherlands to over five years in Italy. Note that across Europe lenders have the right of recourse following repossession; in practice, there are differences on how stringent this right is executed. These gaps are directly reflected in the distribution of the risks between the borrower and the lender. Therefore, it is hardly surprising that in countries like the Netherlands, where the consequences of arrears and repossessions are fast and severe, the number of households with payment difficulties is consistently lower than in other countries. The reverse is also true: in countries with a strong tradition of consumer protection (e.g. in Southern Europe) lenders are not prepared – precisely because of this tradition – to grant high mortgages to owner-occupiers.

All European governments provide general support for needy households through the social security system. However, the conditions, level and duration of this support vary widely from country to country. In an increasing number of countries (including France and the UK), the government promotes self-protection by obliging mortgage-holders to take out insurance against arrears due to long-term illness and invalidity.

Although, the diversity of the issues addressed in this section makes it difficult to sketch a more comprehensive picture, two trends are clearly visible: convergence across Europe in non-financial regulations and conservatism in the system of housing provision (Ball and Grilli, 1997).

3.4 Differences and similarities amongst homeowners and borrowers

Next to the institutional context, differences in characteristics of (recent) buyers may help to explain the distinct pattern of mortgage take-up and the apparent diversity of the risk attitude of borrowers.

The characteristics of borrowers are portrayed here in three steps. First, Figure 3.1 depicts the share of owner-occupiers, borrowers and recent buyers in each country. Second, in Figure 3.2, the household profile of homeowners and recent buyers is described in more detail and compared across countries. The focus in the third part of this section is on households in arrears. Who are they, and which households are most at risk?

Differences in homeownership rates, ranging from just 50% in Denmark to over 75% in Italy, are well known and have been discussed above (Section 1.1) and elsewhere. The share of borrowers also differs across countries (see Section 3.2); here Italy combines the highest homeownership rates with the lowest share of borrowers (13%), while both Denmark and the Netherlands have low, but rising, homeownership rates coupled with a high numbers of borrowers. There is less difference in the share of recent buyers, shown in Figure 3.1

Figure 3.1 Homeownership rates, share of borrowers and share of recent buyers amongst them* (EU6, 2003)

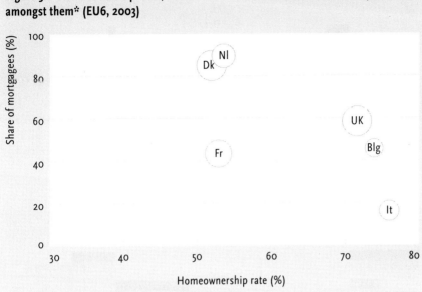

Source: European Community Household Panel

* Percentage of all owner-occupiers that bought their present property in the last year (depicted by the size of the circles/point).

Note the low number of recent buyers in Italy and Belgium, reflecting the old idea that households in these countries tend to buy only once in their housing career, while households in Northwest Europe are far more mobile.

by the size of the circles, but the stories behind this are quite dissimilar. The proportion of recent buyers among Italian homeowners is, for instance, relatively high because Italian homeowners tend to repay their mortgage debt as soon as possible;, leaving a relatively small proportion of borrowers (and a relatively high proportion of recent buyers amongst them). The high number of recent buyers in, for instance, the UK is due to a high mobility rate (every 7 to 8 years, compared to just once every 20 years in Italy).

Figure 3.2 shows the household characteristics of homeowners and recent buyers. The profiles are based on six attributes: age, income, household size (i.e. percentage of singles), source of income (i.e. percentage of employed), the share of single-earners, and finally, the percentage of highly educated members in both groups. Together, these factors form a distinctive risk profile for the average homeowner/recent buyer. The results are presented as z-scores to facilitate a cross-country comparison between the different factors.

The foremost conclusion that can be drawn from Figure 3.2 is that – compared with the European average (EU6) – households in the UK are older, have a higher income, have a relatively higher proportion of singles[27] (and in combination), are more often single-earners, and have a relatively high level of

---

27 In accordance with the demographic patterns discussed in Section 3.1.

Figure 3.2 Some characteristics of homeowners and recent buyers (EU6, z-score, 2001)

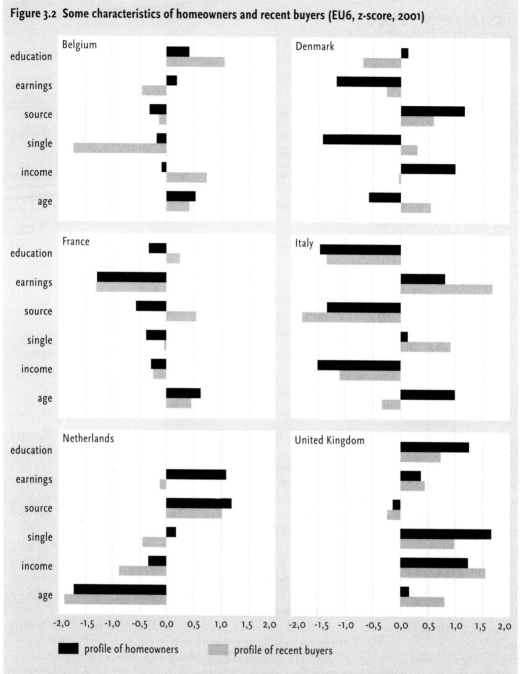

Source: European Community Household Panel

A positive z-score indicates that the paradigmatic case representing the 'average household' in a specific country scores higher than the European average (EU6).

education = the percentage of households with higher education; earnings = the share of single-earners; source = source of income, i.e. percentage of buyers employed; single = household size, i.e. percentage of singles; income = income and age = age head of household education. All these characteristics imply that their risk profile is better than the average 'European' homeowner is. On the downside, their source of income seems to be less secure as their jobs tend to be more precarious (self-employed). Given the high proportion of borrowers and recent buyers, the profile is quite similar for both.

The same type of analysis can be conducted for other countries. The main results can be sketched as follows. Belgian homeowners score an 'average' profile; only the percentage of singles among recent buyers is considerably lower than elsewhere. Therefore, they seem to be playing safe, given the low mortgage take-up in Belgium. Italian homeowners, on the other hand, have a rather high-risk profile: their income is low and uncertain (high share of non-employed and low educated). Even the risk profile for French homeowners, notwithstanding their low mortgage take-up, seems to be relatively high, although not as distinctive as for Italian homeowners. Danish homeowners are relatively well off, also due to the low number of single-earners. Finally, Dutch homeowners are rather young and have a low income, but income-security is relatively high[28].

It seems that high mortgage take-up in some countries, including the Netherlands and the UK, is partly compensated by a better profile for (prospective) homeowners. In most countries, the profile for recent buyers is not much different from the profile for borrowers in general (as to be expected).

Households at risk
Table 3.7 reports the three measurements of unsustainable homeownership mentioned earlier: households experiencing housing costs as a heavy burden, the incidence of mortgage arrears, and the number of repossessions. It is clear from Table 3.8 that for every household in arrears there are – on average – eight households who experience their housing costs as a heavy financial burden. Ultimately, less than 5% of them will face repossession[29].

The characteristics of households in arrears have been well researched (see Neuteboom and Dol (2005) for an overview). Most researchers use a logistic regression approach to identify households that are more at risk; i.e. the in-arrears group is compared with the not-in-arrears group. In these analyses, a set of socio-economic characteristics is used as explanatory variables. Burrows (1998), for instance, used this procedure for the UK while Neuteboom and Dol (2005) performed a similar analysis on a cross-country basis and confirmed earlier country-by-country studies. Households in low-income groups

---

28 The ECHP does not offer reliable information on the education level of Dutch households. Additional analysis on the Dutch Housing Need Survey reveals that both borrowers and recent buyers are relatively well educated.
29 Note that this implies that most arrears are just temporary; mainly because households in arrears were able to adopt strategies to overcome their problems (or a positive change in income or interest rates occurred).

Table 3.7 Some measurements of unsustainable homeownership (per 1,000 outstanding mortgages) (EU6, 2001)

	Housing costs = heavy burden	Mortgage arrears	Repossessions[1]
Belgium	224	38	0.16
Denmark	81	5	0.77
France	163	17	n.a.
Italy	450[2]	51	n.a.
Netherlands	11	8	0.3
UK	54	9	1.61

Source: European Community Household Panel, Neuteboom (2002), Housing Statistics in the EU

1. Average 1996-2001; 2. Italian homeowners are rather pathetic anyway, more than 5 million households complained about high housing costs even when they consist only of local taxes and maintenance.

are significantly more at risk than others; so are single parents (single persons are not at risk; this statistic is partly explainable by the relatively high number of elderly persons with minimum outstanding mortgages). Also overrepresented are self-employed households – because of insecurity of income – and households with a low educational level (diminishing labour opportunities). Obviously, households with other debts are also significantly more at risk. Finally, somewhat surprisingly perhaps, recent buyers do not run more risks than non-movers do. Though, on average, they have more outstanding debt than non-movers do, the risk-assessment procedures applied by lenders ensure that, in the short term, the debt-service ratio is within limits. Therefore, arrears are unlikely. However, as time passes, the probability of unforeseen events increases, and hence the probability of arrears[30].

3.5 National mortgage markets

A host of rules and regulations governed mortgage markets in Europe until the mid-1980s and early 1990s (Bakker, 1996). A lot has changed since. Financial deregulation, partly 'forced' through EU directives, has brought about major changes in the (inter)national mortgage markets. The UK started deregulating its financial system in the early 1980s, followed later by other countries. The policy changes included the abolition of interest-rate ceilings and the relaxation of quantitative credit controls[31] and/or contractual restrictions. From the 1990s onward, independent public bodies carried out financial supervision,

---

30 The analysis does not reveal whether the characteristics of a household in arrears changed for the worse after taking out the mortgage, but it does give some indication that borrower characteristics differ across countries and that this difference can (partly) explain the current pattern of unsustainable home-ownership across countries.

31 For instance, in Italy the maximum loan-to-value ratio for secured loans was raised from 50% to 90%.

e.g. the FSA in the UK or the AFM in the Netherlands, see for instance BIS (2006) and EC (2006). These institutions were set up to regulate the financial industry and to protect consumers by, amongst other things, stipulating lending practice (European code of conduct). Barriers preventing (foreign) lenders from entering the mortgage market were also lifted. Governments took a back seat; subsidised mortgages were either abolished or increasingly confined to specific groups. The 1990s saw a wave of mergers and lender privatisations, which increased economies of scale. Finally, the secondary market started to get off the ground, although it should be said that the combined secondary market in Europe is still only a fraction of the size of the secondary market in the USA (EMF, 2004).

All these changes triggered spectacular growth in the mortgage market, not only in terms of outstanding mortgages but also in terms of product variation and in mortgage accessibility for (prospective) homeowners[32]. Despite all of this, the general trend towards liberalisation in Europe has not led to a single integrated European mortgage market. Indeed, the market is still fragmented along national lines. The financial barriers can be gradually overcome but the non-financial barriers (legislation, regulations, subsidy systems etc.) continue to obstruct the evolution of a uniform mortgage market (Stephens, 2000; ECB, 2003). In the end, this inhibits competition, pushes up interest rates and impedes financial innovation (a narrower range of mortgages and hence less choice).

Although the liberalisation has led to a break down of formal rules, lenders in the Netherlands and abroad maintain their own set of rules, governing their lending criteria. Two different systems are being used: risk-based pricing and/or credit rationing. Theoretically, risk-based pricing should be beneficial in the mortgage market, because it allows lenders to price their products more accurately in terms of the (credit) risks incurred by lending to specific households. For instance, a high loan-to-value ratio increases the credit risk and should be priced accordingly (i.e. higher interest rates). With the exception of the UK, risk-based pricing is not common in the 'mortgage industry'.

In continental Europe the most widely applied system is (still) credit rationing. Before the liberalisation, this was regulated by the national government, which sometimes laid down highly specific conditions for the granting of mortgages. Nowadays, though regulations exist in very few countries (see Table 3.10), the internal institutions, such as the level of the maximum debt-service ratio and the credit history of the applicant, are still normative in the market. The aim here is to keep high-risk groups out of the mortgage markets and enforce a uniform interest rate on all borrowers. Effectively, under this

---

32 Of course, rapid economic growth and a steady decline of interest rates contributed to the growth of (national) mortgage markets as well.

system, low-risk borrowers pay for high-risk borrowers. Although, this system does not necessarily lead to higher risks for lenders, it hampers the development of national mortgage markets and prevents high-risk borrowers – such as low-income households – from getting a foot in the door. Sometimes, the system of credit rationing is maintained by government regulations, but more often nowadays lenders are put off by the prospect of losing market share, when risk-based pricing is not the market norm.

The implementation of the Basle II Accord – which introduced new regulatory capital requirements – is expected to increase risk-based mortgage pricing.

Product variation

Above (Section 3.2) I sketched a picture of the mainstream mortgages in the different countries. Obviously, these findings cannot be interpreted only as the result of the choices of owner-occupiers; the options available in each country also play a role. Differences still exist between the countries but are being gradually bridged (see Mercer Oliver Wyman, 2003; 2005, for more details). Table 3.8 presents an overview of the mortgage products that are available in the different countries.

Owner-occupiers in Europe can choose from a whole range of mortgages, from the traditional linear product to the more fashionable investment mortgage. They can also choose between a long-term and a short-term mortgage and opt for a fixed-interest period of anything up to thirty years. There is, however, a wide variation in the types of mortgages available within Europe; for example, over 4,000 products are marketed in the UK, although the differences between them are not always very great (Early, 2005). In many (Southern) European countries, on the other hand, the range is fairly limited for most customers as a lot of mortgage types are available only to low-risk customers[33].

In the 1990s, the mortgage product range expanded in the wake of the deregulation of the finance markets. With the exception of Italy, the differences between the countries are now small and are being kept alive by traditions and specific aspects of the institutional context. The expectation is that a greater choice will emerge in Europe and the differences between the countries will gradually fade (Mercer Oliver Wyman, 2003) because of, amongst others, cross-border lending and mergers. However, this does not, imply automatically that the demand for these products will be the same in each country.

Borrowers' accessibility

Nowadays, borrowers have better access to mortgages than in the past. The

---

33 Mortgage contract heterogeneity – over time and across countries – is, of course partly based on different traditions but is also well explainable in terms of differences in funding requirements and regulation (Leece, 2004).

Table 3.8 Mortgage product availability (EU6, 2003)

	Belgium	Denmark	France	Italy	Netherlands	UK
Interest rates (fixed interest rate periods)						
Variable	●	●	●	●	●	●
Referenced	○	●	●	●	●	●
Discounted	○	○	●	●○	○	●
Capped	●	●	●	●○	●	●
Duration						
2-5 years	●	●	●	●	●	●
5-10 years	●	●	●	●	●	●○
10-20 years	●	●	●	●○	●	●○
20+ years	●	●	●○	●○	●○	○
Mortgage type						
Amortising	●	●	●	●	●	●
Interest only	●○	●○	●	●○	●	●
Flexible	●○	●○	●	●○	●	●

Source: Mercer Oliver Wyman (2003)

● = readily available; ●○ = limited availability; ○ = not available

growth in homeownership rates, the share of borrowers and the average out-standing mortgage debt show that more and more households are finding their way to the mortgage markets.

In general, the range of mortgage products available, as show in table 3.8, is on an individual level more limited. On one hand, lenders do not approve every mortgage type for each customer (credit rationing, see discussion above); the wealthy – in terms of either housing wealth or household income – have more opportunities than for instance first-time buyers. On the other hand, homeowners are choosing quite often the mortgage with the lowest initial costs; setting aside, for instance, short-term repayment mortgages. Although in each country credit constraint borrowers do exist – for instance some first-time buyers – empirical evidence shows that many do not borrow to their maximum limits (Breslaw *et al.*, 1996, see also Chapter 5).

Table 3.9 contains some information on mortgage accessibility for different types of borrowers and/or purposes. High-risk groups such as low-income households and the self-employed are not automatically excluded in all countries (e.g. the Netherlands, the UK) but in the majority of countries, including Belgium and France, many potential high-risk groups are denied access to the mortgage market. Not surprisingly, Mercer Oliver Wyman (2003) concluded that "... *we observe that sub-prime and non-conforming lending (where there are significant differences in price to account for differing risks) is only significant in the UK with all other markets having only an emerging or non-existent high risk lending market*" (ibid, pp. 38). In defence, it would be fair to say that in most countries

Table 3.9 Mortgage accessibility (EU6, 2003)

	Belgium	Denmark	France	Italy	Netherlands	UK
Borrower						
Young (<30 year)	●○	●	●○	●○	●○	●
Older (>50 year)	●○	●	●○	●○	●	●
Low equity	○	○	●	○	●○	●
Self-employed	●○	●	●○	●	●○	●
Credit impaired	●○	●○	●○	●○	●○	●
Purpose						
Second mortgage	●	●	●○	●	●	●
Equity release	●○	●	○	●	●	●

Source: Mercer Oliver Wyman (2003)

● = readily available; ●○ = limited availability; ○ = not available

a subprime market is not yet necessary because (local) governments provide additional guarantees (Section 3.3).

Nevertheless, here as well, things are changing. Financial deregulation and the entrance of new lenders are continuously reshaping the market and slowly bridging the gap between high-access and low-access national mortgage markets.

3.6 Some preliminary conclusions

It is not easy to sketch a clear picture and to produce a ranking-order of the different countries, on mortgage take-up, institutions, (prospective) home-owners or national mortgage markets. In terms of mortgage take-up, it is indeed possible to categorise high debt countries (Denmark, the Netherlands and the UK) versus low debt countries (Belgium, France, Italy); a distinction that is both valid on a macro and micro level. However, the implications in terms of costs and risks for individual homeowners remain obscure.

The reasons are straightforward: there is not one indicator or even a set of indicators, that could objectively capture the differences across countries on any of the four mentioned themes and certainly, the interdependence between those themes cannot adequately be addressed.

Although, the analysis in this chapter does not inform us on the expected costs and associated risks, however, it does informs us that differences on these themes are significantly across countries. It also reveals that the partial effects on costs and risks can be substantive (e.g. housing provision). Therefore, while mortgage take-up in the Netherlands is, by far, the highest in the EU6 (on both a macro and micro level) and consumer protection is just moderate, on the other hand, the analysis also showed that the risk profile of borrowers is better than the 'average' in the EU6 and the housing provision system is relatively generous.

For this study, it is necessary that the full effects of mortgage take-up, institutions, characteristics of (prospective) homeowners and national mortgage markets on the expected net costs and risks be coherently quantified. That way, one can not only compare costs and risks across countries, based on one common denominator, but also determine the underlying risk attitudes.

4 Modelling the ex-ante probabilities of mortgage arrears and repossessions[34, 35]

4.1 Introduction

To evaluate the mortgage choices and choice behaviour of individual home-owners and ultimately their risk attitude, we need a common denominator. Evaluating the outcomes in terms of mortgage contracts will not suffice, since mortgage contracts are often complex and differ in many aspects. What is needed is to redefine mortgage contracts in terms of consequences, hence costs and risks (here: arrears and repossessions). Since, these consequences are not clear (certain) to individual households when they choose from different mortgage contracts, as the future costs (e.g. interest rates) and income are uncertain. It seems that the best way to proceed is to compute the expected costs and risks (the ex-ante approach), *"by effectively accounting for every possible value that each variable could take and weighting each possible scenario by the probability of its occurrence"* (Vose, 1996, p. 8). This can be achieved by applying a Monte Carlo Simulation.

A Monte Carlo Simulation (MCS) is a 'forward-looking' analytical method, based on the historical probability distributions of parameters. It is particularly useful for tackling path-dependent or history-dependent problems (Vose, 1996; Trigeorgis, 1996). MCS is a method for iteratively evaluating a deterministic model, using sets of random numbers as input. It is often used when the model is complex, non-linear, or involves more than just a few uncertain parameters. Generally, the MCS approach consists of the following steps (Boyle et al., 1997): first, it simulates scenarios of the underlying institutional variables (here: interest rates, house prices, household income etc.) over the relevant time horizon, and second, it computes the discounted value of – in this case – the annual net costs or debt-service ratio. The annual net costs and the debt-service ratio are then no longer characterised by one – i.e. the most likely – outcome, but by a probability distribution of all possible outcomes. The variation in the results can then serve as a basis for determining the risk (Trigeorgis, 1996).

Within the context of mortgage choice models a simulation approach has been applied by for instance Milevsky (2001), Templeton et al. (1996) and Tucker (1991). Their aim was to study choices of households between fixed and adjustable interest rates. Their models were rather static, calculating the net present value difference for different types of mortgages with just one ran-

---

34 Some of the more technical details are left out of the core text of this chapter; these issues are added, as an appendix (technical note), at the end of this chapter.

35 An earlier version of this chapter was published in Neuteboom (2003).

dom variable: mortgage interest rates. The basic assumption in these models is that households follow the costs minimisation hypothesis (Breslaw et al., 1996): households that were not constrained by affordability considerations were to assume choosing the mortgage with the lowest expected cost over the full duration of the mortgage while constraint borrowers would focus on the immediate, first-year, costs. Given the finite nature of these models, I will not discuss them here in-depth, but acknowledge that these models have paved the way for a newer generation of models (see Leece, 2004 for an overview).

The model presented here, is in line with the research by Yang et al. (1998), Capozza et al. (1998) and Campbell and Cocco (2003), although the usage and exact specification are quite divergent. Yang et al. and Capozza et al., both used a simple stochastic model to research the probabilities of mortgage default under different conditions, i.e. fundamental changes in interest rates and house prices or a different set of initial premises; in other words, different loan-to-value ratios. The model of Capozza et al. consisted of a house price model and an interest rate model. Arrears occurred when the total expected cost of the mortgage was higher than the actual house prices (i.e. the analysis was based on the equity hypothesis discussed in Chapter 2.3). Yang et al. extended the model by incorporating an income model as well. They shared the same interest as Capozza et al. but their starting point was the ability-to-pay hypothesis, so default occurred when the housing/mortgage costs-to-income ratio was higher than a given hurdle rate. Their model offered a much better explanation of historical arrears.

In this research, the aim is to model the costs and risks of different types of mortgages in order to get a clear picture of the choice patterns of home-owners. The study by Campbell and Cocco came close to this. They used a stochastic model to investigate, in the US, how the optimal choice of a home-owner for a fixed-rate as opposed to a variable-rate mortgage was conditioned. They enhanced the models described above with a more sophisticated income model; in their version of the income model the macro-uncertainty for household income (economic growth, inflation) was modelled together with the micro-uncertainty (household dissolution, unemployment).

The model presented below (Sections 4.2 and 4.3) differs in many respects from theirs, mainly because it focuses more explicitly on the institutional context as well as the different mortgage and household characteristics[36].

---

36 Of course, the exact specification of the income, house price and interest models differs as well, but these differences are rather small, certainly compared with Campbell and Cocco and Yang et al.

4.2 Model specification

The simulation model I used in this research to compute the expected costs and risks of a mortgage consists of five sub-models (see Figure 2.2), which simulate interest rates, household income, house prices, stock market developments and inflation. In this section, these five sub-models will be discussed one by one.

Interest rates
First, I start with modelling the spot rate (1 month) followed by the derivation of the interest rate for different maturities (yield curve). The basic model[37] applied here is the stochastic differential equation:

$$(1) \quad dr_t = \lambda(\mu - r_t)dt + \sigma\sqrt{r_{t-1}}\,dX_1$$

in which λ is the speed of adjustment of the short-term actual interest rate r_t to the long-term mean μ and $\sigma\sqrt{r_{t-1}}$ is the implied volatility. When $\mu > \%_2$, interest rates remain positive. The last term dX_1 is a random variable drawn from a normal distribution with the following properties:

$$dX_1 = \varphi\sqrt{dt}$$
$$E[dX_1] = 0$$
$$E[dX_1^2] = 1$$

The model is a mean-reverting process ($\lambda(\mu - r_t)dt$), implying that if $r_t > \mu$, interest rates will move down on average, although the random term $\sigma\sqrt{r_{t-1}}dX_1$ can make interest rates rise, on balance, even when they are above average (and vice versa). This model can be used to simulate different scenarios for possible future interest rates (paths) for the total duration of the mortgage.

So far, the process has yielded the expected spot interest rate, i.e. the interest rate for loans with duration of one month. From there, we must derive the interest rates for loans with different maturities and fixed-term periods as well as the appropriate interest rates for residential mortgages. By utilising a default-free discount bond model $P(t,T)$ (see equation 1b), we can derive the – theoretical – equilibrium interest rates for different maturities (Rebonato, 1998; Chen et al., 1995), in short the yield-curve:

$$(1b) \quad rt_t = \frac{-\ln(P(t,T))}{(T-t)}$$

---

[37] The so-called CIR model is named after Cox, Ingersoll and Ross (1985). See Rebonato (1998) for further details.

$$P(t,T) = A(t,T)e^{-r_tB(t,T)}$$

and

$$A(t,T) = \left\{ \frac{\phi_1 e^{\phi_2\tau}}{\phi_2\left[e^{\phi_2\tau}-1\right]+\phi_1} \right\}^{\phi_3}, \quad B(t,T) = \frac{e^{\phi_2\tau}-1}{\phi_2\left[e^{\phi_2\tau}-1\right]+\phi_1}$$

$$\phi_1 = \sqrt{\lambda^2 + 2\sigma^2}, \quad \phi_2 = \frac{\lambda+\phi_1}{2}, \quad \phi_3 = \frac{2\lambda\mu}{\sigma^2}, \quad \tau = T-t$$

in which rt_t represents the interest rate in year t with a fixed interest period of T. The parameters λ, σ, μ follow from equation 1. Hence, the yield curve is a function of the short-term rate r_t.

An increase in the actual interest rate increases yields for all maturities, but the effect is greater for shorter maturities. Similarly, as $r_t > \mu$, all yields increase but the effect is greater for shorter durations. Indeed, it is possible for a downward sloping yield curve to arise, which implies that the 'market' expects lower interest rates (lower inflation) in the near future. A decreasing yield curve is not only a theoretical option, but also a rare, temporal, phenomenon that occurs in practice[38].

From the actual yield curve, it is easy to derive the interest rates for a mortgage. In the model, the interest rate calculated with equations 1a and 1b is supplemented with a spread, i.e. the difference between mortgage interest and the interest on a comparable government bond. This spread itself is a function of both the short-term rate and the fixed-interest period, being relatively low when the short-term rates are below the long-term mean and relatively high when fixed periods increase. This means that the yield curve for mortgage rates shifts proportionally when interest rates are low while the slope of the curve decreases with higher interest rates.

The model also takes account of interest rate conversion after the agreed fixed-interest period have ended and incorporate the possibility of early prepayment as well (i.e. checking whether it is profitable to make an early prepayment on the loan, given the different costs and penalties).

For an illustration see Figure 4.1, where the different mortgage interest rates are derived from one estimated interest (spot) rate path. This figure is based on the Dutch setting.

Net household income

Net household income is determined by a whole range of factors: at the macro level by general trends in income, based on economic growth, and at micro level by, for example, changes in the status in the labour market (e.g. redundancy or promotion) and/or demographic factors (e.g. divorce). Changes at the

---

38 See, for instance, the period 1991-1992 in the Netherlands and the period 1997-1998 in the UK.

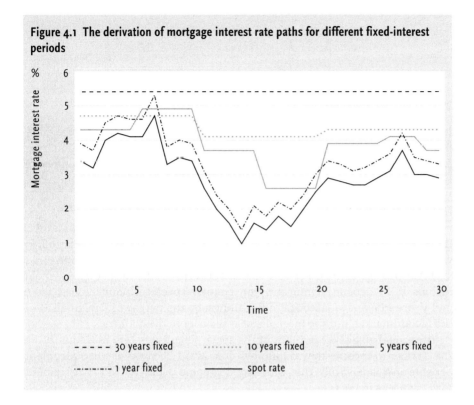

Figure 4.1 The derivation of mortgage interest rate paths for different fixed-interest periods

----- 30 years fixed   ·········· 10 years fixed   ———— 5 years fixed

·-·-·-·-·- 1 year fixed   ———— spot rate

macro level might have a relatively modest effect on individual household in-comes, but changes at the micro level may have a deep impact.

The literature offers two basic models to define and estimate develop-ments of net household income:

■ a 'mover-stayer' model in which the household income either remains the same ('stayer') or takes a clear upward or downward turn as a result of pro-motion or redundancy ('mover');
■ a purely random walk model (like equations 3 and 4, see below).

Since we know from earlier research that net household income is the most important determinant of unsustainable homeownership (see Chapter 2), it is vital that the model captures both macro economic variations and micro income changes. The latter includes loss of job or retirement, but also demo-graphic transformations such as divorce; changes that can be expected to have a huge impact on household income and hence on the sustainability of the mortgage payments.

Dutta et al. (2001) have developed a model, which may be regarded as a synthesis of the two basic models. This model fits perfectly within the con-ceptual model, because it takes account of both macro and micro changes. It is a binominal model in which households either do not experience a leap in net income (+ or -/-) – in which case, net household income follows a random walk model – or the other way around. This model is shown in equation 2:

$$(2) \begin{bmatrix} \text{Prob.} & \theta & dy_t = \mu dt + \sigma dX_2 \\ \text{Prob.} & (1-\theta) & dy_t = \tilde{y}_t / y_{t-1} \end{bmatrix}$$

It 'reads' as follows: with probability θ no significant changes will take place in the household income; hence, the household income will change from year to year according to a simple random walk model. Here μ and σ represent the average growth rate and standard deviation (based on historical patterns). With probability $(1-\theta)$ a significant positive or negative change will occur in the household income. In these cases, the model assigns the household a new net household income $\tilde{y}_t$, which is drawn randomly from the income distribution. The new household income is $\tilde{y}_t$ drawn from the distribution $N(\tilde{\mu}_t, \tilde{\sigma}_t)$, in which $\tilde{\mu}_t$ and $\tilde{\sigma}_t$ are the mean and variance of the recurrent distribution.

Note that we can expect both the probability θ and the new household income $\tilde{y}_t$ to depend significantly on country-specific circumstances; i.e. θ and $\tilde{y}_t$ are influenced, amongst other things, by the degree of deregulation of the labour market and the level of social security in the country.

The model also takes account of the social security system in a country. I.e. the change in income may be limited downward because of unemployment benefits in place, while the anticipated income reduction after retirement may have less impact.

House prices

Trends in house prices do not have a direct influence on the net costs or the affordability of a house. However, they do have a significant effect on the equity risks of a household. The model used here to estimate house prices is a simple random walk model:

$$(3) \ dh_t = \mu dt + \sigma dX_3$$

Here the house price is h_t. The factor μdt is the so-called drift rate while is σdX_3 a normal random variable. In the short term, house price movements are mainly determined by the volatility factor, in the longer term the drift rate gains in importance and the cumulative drift rate tends towards $\sum \mu dt$.

Stock market

The sub-model, which simulates stock market developments takes exactly the same form (and makes the same assumptions) as the house price model and therefore needs no further explanation here:

$$(4) \ dh_t = \mu dt + \sigma dX_4$$

Obviously, stock market developments only come into play if the mortgage is investment-based.

Inflation

The inflation, used for the calculation of the net present values, is derived from the Fisher equation:

$$(1+p_t) = (1+r_t)/(1+i_t)$$

in which p_t represents the real interest rate and i_t represents the inflation. If we assume that the real interest rate ($\bar{p}$) is constant, it follows that:

(5) $i_t = (r_t-\bar{p})/(1+\bar{p})$

Finally, the four sub-models – equations 1 to 4 – are, of course, mutually interdependent, meaning that future developments in interest rates, income, property prices and the stock market are – as in the past – intertwined (for instance, rising interest rates bring down the property prices, ceteris paribus); *"the model therefore must be restricted to prevent it from producing, in any iteration, a scenario that could not physically occur"* (Vose, 1996, p. 191). One way of doing that is by generating the different random numbers $dX_1 - dX_4$ as being multi-correlated. Second, when more than one random number is used in a simulation and the relevant probabilities are rather small (here, for example, the probability of repossessions is expected to be very small), many simulations are required to ensure that the results remain reliable. Then it becomes increasingly important to implement variance-reduction techniques to keep computing time within limits without losing accuracy. Both issues are dealt with in technical note 4.1 at the end of this chapter.

4.3 Calculating the debt-service ratio and the probability of arrears and repossessions

The previous section explained how the scenarios for the exogenous factors are determined. This section will focus on the expected costs and the calculation of the default and equity risks.

The net monthly mortgage payments can be computed based on the scenarios generated by the models 1 to 5 (e.g. developments in interest rates and income), in conjunction with the type of mortgage, household characteristics and the institutional context. The default risks can be deduced based on (monthly) net costs in relation to net household income. The equity risks can then be determined by ascertaining the incidence of payment problems in combination with trends in property prices versus the outstanding mortgage debt.

Expected costs
The net monthly (or annual) costs can be calculated as follows:

$$ME_t = \left[1-\tau(Y_t)\right]r_t MD_t + A_t^* + D_t^* + K_t(MD_t) - S_t(Y_t)$$
$$MD_t = MD_{t-1} - A_t^*$$

in which $\left[1-\tau(Y_t)\right]r_t$ represents the net interest charges; A_t^* and D_t^* the scheduled repayments; $K_t(MD_t)$ the additional costs of a mortgage; and $S_t(Y_t)$ the additional, non-fiscal subsidies. A_t^* and D_t^* depend on the type of mortgage: the model distinguishes between linear, annuity-based, endowment, and investment-based. In linear and annuity-based mortgages, annual payments are made towards the principal throughout the life of the mortgage ($A_t^* > 0$). This system does not apply to the other mortgage types. With endowment and investment-based mortgages the annual payments towards the principal are replaced by contributions to a fund ($D_t^* > 0$), which are then either deposited in a special savings account or used for purchasing shares (funds). The additional charges K_t are directly dependent on the outstanding mortgage debt and relate to the one-off costs (commission, taxes) and the annual obligatory (servicing) costs and/or compulsory insurances. Some households may also be eligible for S_t, i.e. non-fiscal subsidies designed to ease the financial burden of a mortgage. Eligibility for these subsidies usually depends on the household income and sometimes on the composition of the household. Finally, the net present value is calculated from the net annual mortgage payments; this means that the time value of the future payments and (any) returns are taken into account. The result is a probability distribution of the expected mortgage payments, based on the N-scenarios (see also Figure 4.2).

Debt-service ratio
Dividing monthly (annual) net mortgage payments by net household income, as simulated by sub-model 2, shows the development of the debt-service ratio. This ratio is crucial in the analysis, since it is used as a forward indicator of unsustainable homeownership. Like the expected costs, discussed above, the results of the N-scenarios can be regarded as a probability distribution; a fictitious example is shown in Figure 4.2.

The default probabilities can be easily calculated from this distribution and – with some supplementary calculations – so can the repossession rate.

Arrears
Mortgage arrears occur when an owner-occupier is no longer able to meet the financial commitments he has undertaken for the purchase of his home. Arrears may be the result of an unexpected increase in housing costs (due to a rise in the interest rate) or a drop in net household income (due to unemployment, a reduction in working time or a divorce). Not every change in housing costs or income will automatically result in arrears. Owner-occupiers generally have a buffer to absorb any setbacks, but eventually when the debt-service ratio increases, arrears become more likely, until $P(DSR_t \geq \delta)$.

Figure 4.2 Estimated distribution of the debt-service ratio

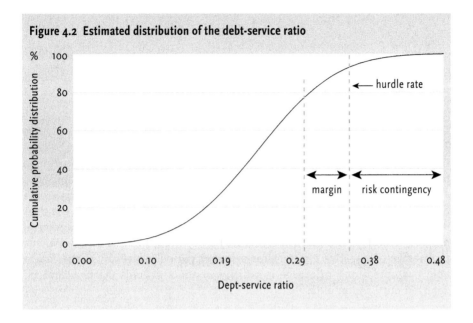

At this point they become unavoidable. Here δ represents the so-called 'hurdle rate', i.e. the debt-service ratio that leads inevitably to unsustainable home-ownership, or more specifically, mortgage arrears. Although one can expect this hurdle rate to be dependent on time, actual net income, and the institutional context, I assume a constant hurdle rate for all countries. In Figure 4.2, this area is labelled 'risk contingency'.

Repossessions
When arrears become long-standing, the household eventually has to move, either voluntarily or because of a compulsory sale. Such households may then be confronted with the added problem of (the risk of) lost capital. Therefore, the probability of being forced to move / being evicted is

$$P(DSR_{t+i..t+n} > \delta)$$

in which $i-n$ is equal to the repossession time in a specific country. The times-cale between the start of mortgage arrears and a compulsory or 'voluntary' sale depends primarily on the legal situation. As mentioned earlier, in the UK, the day of reckoning arrives after only six months of uninterrupted arrears, whereas in some Southern European countries it can take up to five or seven years. The model assumes that if a household is confronted with successive payment arrears during a nationally determined period (ranging from ½ to 6 years, see Table 3.6), the next step is the compulsory or voluntary sale of the property.

   If the sum of the outstanding mortgage debt and the arrears turns out to be higher than the selling price, the household faces (the risk of) capital loss. Earlier, the equity risk was defined as the probability of negative equity, given the existence of mortgage arrears; this is therefore the conditional probability:

$$P(P_t+D_t-MD_t \mid DSR_{t+i..t+n} > \delta)$$

This is not, incidentally, the only situation in which negative equity can arise. The assumption in other cases is that the household in question has at least the opportunity to postpone the sale until a more favourable moment; in these circumstances, there is actually some sort of 'virtual' negative equity.

As property prices tend to rise steadily, the risk of negative equity is obviously greatest when the initial loan is taken out; on the other hand, the prospect of a crisis on the housing market and a downward spiral in the price of property should not be downplayed. In other words, there is still a realistic probability of negative equity after a longer period, especially if the household has opted for a mortgage in which payments towards the principal are deferred until a later date.

4.4 Estimation procedure

Data and empirical methodology

Data on the institutional factors were presented in Chapter 3. The model makes explicit use of:

- mortgage interest tax relief system $[\tau(Y_t)]$;
- non-fiscal subsidies $[S_t]$;
- any additional costs $[K_t MD_t]$ (insurance obligations and closing fees);
- five different types of mortgages;
- mortgage characteristics: duration, fixed-interest period, and prepayment fines;
- financial support for households in arrears (public or private);
- unpaid interest due when in arrears;
- repossession time.

The necessary (minimum) data on household characteristics used in the model was also discussed above (Section 3.4). In what follows, data is used on the income, outstanding mortgage and the loan-to-value, loan-to-income and debt-service ratios.

The different parameters of the model, represented by equations 1-5, were estimated as follows. First, the estimation of the interest model: the basic equation was estimated by using weighted least square, as suggested by Chen *et al.* (1995) (see appendix A for a more comprehensive analysis). Second, the estimation of the income model implied maximum likelihood estimation (see Dutta, 1997) (see Appendix A for further elaboration). Third, in a lognormal representation of the random walk model (used here both for house prices and stock market developments), the drift-rate (σdX) and the implied volatility (μdt) are equal to the mean and variance of the historical developments of house prices and share prices respectively. Therefore, estimation of these parameters is straightforward.

Econometric and statistical results

The results of the estimation procedures of the model represented by sub-models 1-5, as described in this chapter and appendix A are presented in Table 4.1. Note that, when comparing the parameters for a particular model across countries, one should not compare the individual parameter estimates on a one-to-one basis, but the whole parameter set.

Therefore, although the parameters[39] of the income model appear to be quite different across countries, this does not necessarily imply that the expected income growth is equally different. In the UK, for instance, the best fit for the model appears to be high percentage households with a steady income growth (note the kappa[40] of ~84%) in combination with an annual, nominal change in income of just over one percent. If a 'leap' in income occurs, it will bring about an expected income change of nearly 20%.

In the Netherlands, on the contrary, a relatively high percentage of households do experience a significant leap in income every year (~27%) with an expected gain of just six percent. The non-movers group experiences an annual income change of 1.4%. The same story could be told for other households in other countries; overall, households across Europe may expect an annual increase in their income[41].

Some additional comments need to be made on the other models. The same interest model was used for Belgium, France, Italy and the Netherlands because, since the introduction of the euro (and actually well before), the market interest rates have converged to a common level within the euro zone. Separate models were estimated for Denmark and the UK as they still have their own currency and monetary policy. In all the countries in the study, nominal house prices rose by six or seven percent (the high figures for Italy and the UK reflect high inflation in the 1970s and 1980s). House prices are highly volatile in Italy, the Netherlands and the UK. In the UK this stems from high volatility in the short-run (falling house prices are not uncommon) while in the Netherlands, it is the result of a one-time bust in the housing market (early 1980s) and a boom at the end of the twentieth century. The estimation of the stock market developments is based on the AEX (Dutch stock exchange).

---

39 The model was simultaneously estimated for households with a low and with a high income (below or above the median). For further background, see Appendix A. Note that for all households the variability of the household income is higher for the higher income groups. This is due, amongst others, to the instability of the household itself and hence its income.

40 Kappa in this model represents not only changes in socio-economic position but also – more implicitly – models the changes in household structures; hence the estimated kappa is substantially lower than in the Dutta study.

41 Partial simulation of the income model shows that expected income change in all countries is positive: the expected yearly real income changes are estimated for Belgium as 0.34%, Denmark 0.44%, France 0.63%, Italy 0.04%, the Netherlands 0.53%, and for the UK 0.16%.

Table 4.1 Estimated parameters of the interest, income, house price and stock market model

	Belgium	Denmark	France	Italy	Netherlands	UK
Income model						
Kappa (*low income group*)	0.8960	0.8550	0.8650	0.9030	0.7310	0.8380
Kappa (*high income group*)	0.6470	0.4650	0.6340	0.7890	0.5370	0.6210
Mean (*non-mover*)	0.0160	0.0050	0.0238	0.0177	0.0146	0.0103
Implied volatility (*non-mover*)	0.0453	0.0395	0.0280	0.0222	0.0198	0.0155
Mean (*mover, log*)	10.3780	10.6270	10.3510	10.0280	10.2990	10.3120
Volatility (*mover, log*)	0.0690	0.0550	0.1970	0.2010	0.0870	0.2650
Interest model[1]						
Mean-reversion level	0.0390	0.0440	.	.	.	0.0450
Implied volatility	0.0410	0.0330	.	.	.	0.0460
Reversion speed	0.2395	0.2801	.	.	.	0.3834
Spread (av.)	0.0100	0.0070	0.0050	0.0150	0.0040	0.0110
Market price of risk	-0.0358	0.0217	.	.	.	0.0255
House prices model						
Mean	0.0657	0.0720	0.0717	0.1180	0.0749	0.1147
Implied volatility	0.0654	0.0829	0.0661	0.1663	0.1017	0.1102
Stock market model[2]						
Mean	.	.	.	.	0.0671	.
Implied volatility	.	.	.	.	0.2106	.
Administration costs	.	.	.	.	0.0100	.
Inflation	0.0188	0.0221	0.0180	0.0315	0.0282	0.0259

Sources: Interest rates: monthly data from 1990:1-2004:12, "1 month AIBOR/EURIBOR interest rate", and "end month sterling Interbank lending rate, mean LIBID/LIBOR". Income: annual data from 1994-2001, European Community Household Panel. House Prices: annual data from 1971-2002, Bank for International Settlements. Stock market: annual data from 1961-2002, AEX

1. France, Italy and the Netherlands are all considered to have the same parameter set as Belgium.
2. All countries have the same parameter set as the Netherlands.

Since this sub-model is only relevant for investment mortgages, which have a substantial share of the market only in the Netherlands, this assumption does not seem over-ambitious. Finally, all other data used in the model, are shown and discussed in Tables 3.4 to 3.7.

4.5 First results: the costs and risks of a mortgage

Table 4.2 shows the costs and risks of a mortgage in the different countries. The calculation is based on the household characteristics of a recent buyer and the prevailing institutional context. Both are discussed in the previous

Table 4.2 Costs and implied risks of a typical mortgage of € 100,000 (EU6, recent buyers, 2003)

	Belgium	Denmark	France	Italy	Netherlands	UK
Expected costs (€)						
Mean	137,897	124,974	137,889	125,957	113,344	147,472
Trimmed mean	137,920	124,977	137,934	125,495	113,795	147,612
Minimum	124,631	122,198	129,283	119,681	59,624	103,787
Maximum	149,606	127,524	143,436	160,485	135,229	187,553
90%-percentile	142,488	126,011	140,645	128,757	123,180	171,051
Risks (€)						
Standard deviation	3,570	814	2,122	3,899	8,659	19,765
Semi-variance	2,496	569	1,443	3,498	5,349	13,516
Arrears (%, annualised)	--	--	1.73	4.79	1.22	3.10
Repossession (%, annualised)	--	--	0.21	1.33	0.43	2.08
Negative equity (€)	--	--	--	--	--	--

The expected costs of a mortgage of € 100,000 are equal to the mean of the simulated distribution of all possible outcomes (in net present value terms); the other variable gives some additional information on the shape of that distribution. The default % (and the repossession %) indicates the yearly ex-ante probability of default (or being repossessed). Note that these figures in this table are based on the analysis of the paradigmatic case representing the average borrower. Because on a micro level the correlation between mortgage take-up and income may be higher than on a aggregate level, these figures overestimate the default and repossession percentages.

chapter. The mortgage contract specifications represent the typical mortgage (mix) chosen in a country. For instance, in Belgium the typical mortgage consists of a mix of annuity and serial mortgages with a relatively long duration and a fixed-interest period while, in the Netherlands, it consists of a combination of investment and interest-rate-only mortgages with longer duration and shorter fixed-interest periods. For the sake of a genuine comparison, a nominal mortgage of € 100,000 was used.

The expected costs of these mortgages range from € 113,344 in the Netherlands, closely followed by Denmark, to more than € 147,000 in the UK. These differences can be largely traced back to differences in the institutional context, i.e. mortgage interest tax relief. The range between minimum and maximum (expected) costs is quite significant in the Netherlands and the UK. This fits in, of course, with the preference of Dutch and English homeowners for investment mortgages and, in the UK in particular, for mortgages with variable interest rates. Both lead to greater variability in the expected mortgage costs. Mortgage risks can be presented in two different ways. Following on from the discussion in Chapter 2, mortgage risk constitutes uncertainty about both the future mortgage costs and the specific mortgage risk: default and the risk of being repossessed.

Uncertainty about expected mortgage costs is addressed in Table 4.2, presented by the standard deviation and the semi-variance (see technical note 4.2 at the end of this chapter). The results show that the variance is moderate in most countries, with the exception of the Netherlands and the UK (the reasons for this discrepancy are discussed above). Secondly, Table 4.2 shows the risk of default (mortgage arrears), the probability of repossession, and ultimately, the expected negative equity. Remember that the results here are based on a country-specific mortgage contract with a nominal value of €100,000. Since the default and the repossession risk depend heavily on the level and changes of household income in relation to the mortgage costs, the absolute value of these risks are not very informative. Therefore, the discussion of these issues will be delayed until after the presentation of the cost-and-risk equivalent of actual mortgage take-up (Table 5.3).

Finally, it should be noted that the results presented here are based on a paradigmatic case representing the 'average' borrower in a country. Since mortgage take-up and net income differ according to household, one can expect the ratio at micro-level to be better geared than at meso-level presented here; hence the risks shown in Table 4.2 constitute probably a maximum.

Technical notes to Chapter 4

Note 4.1 Random number generator

The practical value of any Monte Carlo Simulation is limited by the convergence of the method, i.e. by the number of simulations that are needed to obtain reliable results. Standard Monte Carlo Simulation implies choosing randomly a series of points $x_1..x_n$ from a standard normal distribution and computing $F(x)$. According to the central limit theorem, the average of the values of $F(x_1..x_n)$ should converge. In the model presented in this chapter $x_1..x_n$ are distributed in a multidimensional space; the number of dimensions is equal to the number of random variables (4).

The four sub-models described in this chapter are mutually dependent, meaning that future developments in interest rates, income, property prices and the stock market are correlated. Therefore, we must correct the model for illogical outcomes, i.e. situations that cannot occur under normal circumstances. One way of doing so is to generate the different random numbers $X_1..X_n$ as multi-correlated. Table 4.3 presents the correlation matrix between the four dependent variables.

To make the model more useful[42], convergences must be speeded up (variance reduction). This can be achieved in several ways. One possibility is to make the distribution of the random numbers as similar to the standard normal distribution as possible. This is done by applying the antithetic variables method, which uses not only every random number drawn from the standard normal distribution but also the opposite. Consequently, the distribution is

---

42 The number of iterations grows exponentially with the number of random variables in the model.

Table 4.3 Correlation matrix between interest rates, shares, house prices, and income (EU6)

	Belgium	Denmark	France	Italy	Netherlands	UK
Interest/shares	0.17	-0.04	0.17	0.17	0.17	-0.05
Interest/house prices	-0.29	-0.50	0.24	0.29	-0.41	-0.13
Interest/income	0.38	-0.04	0.31	0.34	0.18	0.32
Shares/house prices	-0.27	0.06	-0.35	-0.32	-0.25	-0.29
Shares/income	-0.18	-0.05	-0.33	-0.17	0.10	-0.08
House price/income	0.17	0.00	0.66	0.46	0.32	0.29

Source: see Table 4.2

completely symmetrical around zero. Another way of increasing the convergence rate is to use sequences of random numbers, which are more uniformly spread (quasi-random numbers).

Here I used the 'Mersenne Twister' random number generator (version 2.01); this module generates quasi-random numbers while applying an antithetic method and correcting for multi-correlation (see Marsumoto and Nishimura (1998) for further details).

The empirical error was computed in order to assess the precision of the results and to compare the convergence of standard Monte Carlo Simulation with the version described above. The simulation results were divided into ten blocks of equal size; the standard deviation of each set of blocks was used as the empirical error. The results are shown in Figure 4.3 (note that the two methods converge when the number of iterations is higher).

For the main results presented in this chapter and the next, I used a sequence of N = 2,500 simulations[43].

Note 4.2 Semi-variance

The most obvious and most used criterion for risk determination is the variance (or the standard deviation). Standard portfolio analysis shows that a unique arrangement of investment alternatives is possible in a so-called mean-variance framework. This applies mutatis mutandis to the mirror-image issue of the costs and risks of mortgages, the subject of this study. The standard deviation as a criterion also implies, however, that a positive weight is accorded to outcomes below the mean. It may be assumed that an owner-occupier with an aversion to risk-taking will 'fear' higher average mortgage costs and see lower mortgage costs as a bonus. Therefore, not all uncertainties imply a risk (see Chapter 2). Ideally, the risk criterion should consider this. The semi-variance is, in that case, a good alternative (Eftekhari et al., 2000). The semi-variance is an asymmetric indicator and is defined as the sum of

---

[43] In the next chapter, I calculate and compare the costs and risks of different mortgage types, sometimes with just a minor effect on expected costs, default rates etcetera. In order to prevent the empirical error from exceeding the expected difference of different alternative options, the number of cases must be relatively high to get valid results. Hence 2,500 simulations, leading to an empirical error of less than 0,5 percent.

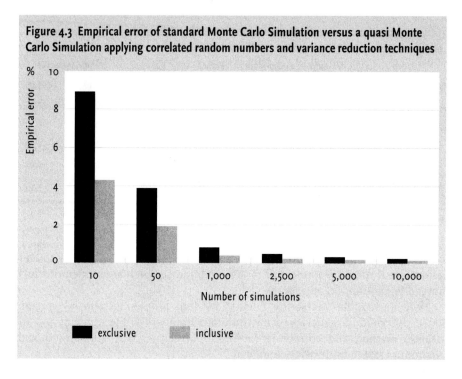

Figure 4.3 Empirical error of standard Monte Carlo Simulation versus a quasi Monte Carlo Simulation applying correlated random numbers and variance reduction techniques

the squared mean differences insofar as the net mortgage repayments are above the mean. If C_i stands for costs, while $\overline{C}$ stands for expected costs, i.e. the mean of the distribution, the semi-variance sv can be computed as:

$$sv = \frac{1}{N} \sum_{i=1}^{N} min[0, C_i - \overline{C}]^2$$

5 Optimal mortgage choice and risks attitudes of borrowers[44, 45]

5.1 Introduction

With the model designed and discussed in the previous chapter it is possible to calculate the expected mortgage costs and (ex-ante) risks, given the typical mortgage characteristics, the profile of the (prospective) borrowers and the institutional setting.

In this chapter, the model is extended to assess the risk attitude of a borrower. Recapping on the discussion in Chapter 2 on the derivation of the risk attitude from actual behaviour, we need to be clear that it is not the stated attitude that matters, but the revealed attitude based on actual choice-behaviour. The idea is to ascertain the attitude of borrowers by comparing their chosen option (i.e. mortgage contracts) in terms of costs and risks, hence incorporating the effect of institutions and different household and mortgage characteristics with all the other available alternatives. This will make it possible to evaluate whether the chosen mortgage contract is optimal and to ascertain if the borrower chooses an option with a low or high-risk profile.

This chapter starts by explaining the methodology (Section 5.2). In Section 5.3, the focus shifts to the costs and risks of the different options within each country. Finally, in Section 5.4, the prevailing risk attitudes of borrowers, subdivided into various categories, are identified and discussed.

5.2 Measuring risk attitudes

Figure 5.1 depicts three steps, which demonstrate how the risk attitude is measured in this thesis. First, the costs and risks – the semi-variance – for the entire range of mortgage contracts on offer on the market are calculated with the model described in the previous chapter. Once calculated, the results in terms of costs and risks embody the relevant institutional context and differences in household characteristics.

It is easily seen from Figure 5.1 (top figure) that some options represent lower costs or lower risks, or both.

An option (mortgage contract) is considered inefficient if other options are available, that offer both lower costs and lower risks. If this is not the case, the original option is regarded as efficient. The efficient options are the ones a rational decision-maker should choose. In Figure 5.1 (second drawing), a line, called the 'efficiency frontier', visualises these efficient options. Note that the

---

44 Some of the more technical details are left out of the core text of this chapter; these issues are added, as an appendix (technical note), at the end of this chapter.

45 An earlier version of this chapter was published in Neuteboom (2005).

Figure 5.1 Measuring risk attitudes I

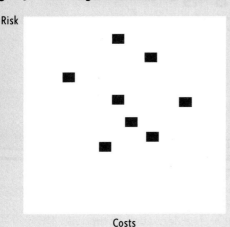

Risk

Costs

Step 1

Calculate the expected costs and
risk – here represented by the
semi variance – of all mortgage
options available (supply
restrictions!) for a homeowner/
decision-maker.

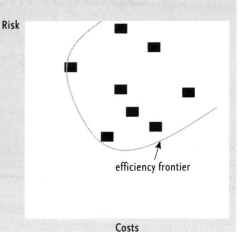

Risk

efficiency frontier

Costs

Step 2

Calculate the efficiency frontier,
i.e. a line representing the
options available with the
lowest costs and risks for the
homeowner/decision-maker.

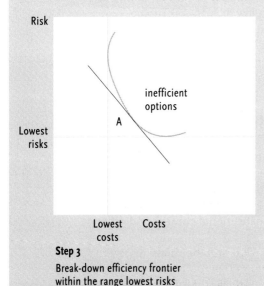

Risk

inefficient
options

A

Lowest
risks

Lowest   Costs
costs

Step 3

Break-down efficiency frontier
within the range lowest risks
and lowest costs.

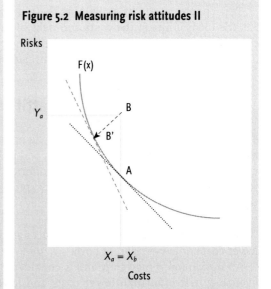

Figure 5.2 Measuring risk attitudes II

Risks

$F(x)$

Y_a

B

B'

A

$X_a = X_b$

Costs

exact shape of the efficiency-frontier is dependent on the product range available. In the lowest Figure, this efficiency frontier is broken down within the
range of lowest costs – lowest risks (see technical note 5.1 at the end of this
chapter for the derivation of the efficiency frontier). The risk attitude is simply derived from the efficiency frontier, i.e. it is equal to the slope of the curve
tangent to the chosen option.

In the real world, not every borrower will choose an option on the efficiency frontier; perhaps caused by unawareness of the option or because the transaction costs for altering the mortgage contract are too high[46]. The distance between the chosen option and the nearest option on the efficiency frontier is a measurement of inefficiency, i.e. an indicator of how much is to be gained if an option is chosen on the efficiency frontier[47].

To illustrate this point, the last drawing in Figure 5.1 is replicated and expanded in Figure 5.2. Here, option A lies on the efficiency frontier $F(x)$; so, by definition, the choice is optimal. The risk attitude in this case is equal to $F'(x_a)$. However, what happens if the borrower chooses option B? Clearly, this option is inefficient (suboptimal) since $F(x_b) \neq y_b$. In this case, the risk attitude of the borrower can be derived by transposing point B to a fictitious point B' on $F(x)$, i.e. a linear transformation so that $y_b - z = F(x_b - z)$. Then the risk attitude can be easily derived as $F'(x_b - z)$. The proportion z can be used to measure the extent of the inefficiency (see also technical note 5.2 at the end of this chapter).

5.3 An assessment of the costs and risks of different mortgages and their alternatives

This section assesses the costs and risks of different mortgages and their alternatives. Although most mortgage contracts are now available in all six European countries (see Section 3.5), this does not necessarily imply that they are available to all customers. Certainly, in Southern European countries, investment and interest-only mortgages are available only to a limited extent for the average borrower. Hence, they are eliminated from the set of available options in these countries. On the other hand, credit constraints imposed on borrowers (i.e. the debt-service ratio should remain below 35%) mean that in high-lending countries (e.g. the Netherlands and the UK) serial loans is not an option either (see discussion in Section 3.5).

Table 5.1 sums up the different mortgage products, which were used in the consecutive analysis. It shows a combination of five mortgage types (the serial and annuity mortgage, the savings and investment mortgage and the interest-only mortgage), a short or long duration (20 and 30 years respectively), and three different fixed-interest periods (monthly interest rates, 10-year variable and 20/30-years fixed); altogether 30 combinations.

---

46 Therefore, not every new mortgage contract innovation will gain immediate support, nor do people respond to changes in their personal circumstances (a new job, household dissolution, etc.) by remortgaging.

47 Note that small inefficiencies can last quite long given the costs of remortgaging. Hence, we can expect inefficiencies to be lower for recent buyers than for non-movers.

Table 5.1 Assessment categories

Mortgage type	Duration	Fixed interest period
• Serial mortgage	• 30 years	• Fixed
• Annuity mortgage	• 20 years	• 10 years
• Savings mortgage		• Variable
• Investment mortgage		
• Interest-only mortgage		

Actual choice: combination of different types (see Table 3.4 for an overview)

In the remainder of this section, first, the cost-and-risk equivalent of actual mortgage take-up is discussed, followed by a presentation of the costs and risks of all available alternative mortgage contracts. Note that the analysis in this section focuses on recent buyers only.

Actual choice: mix of different mortgage types
Table 5.2 presents the actual costs and risks for recent buyers (the table is comparable with Table 4.2). These figures show the actual expected costs and some risk measurement for the average recent buyers in the different countries. In contrast with the results in Table 4.2 – based on a mortgage of €100,000 – the results here are based on exact amount households actually take-up (see last row).

Clearly, the costs and risks of actual mortgage take-up vary considerably between countries. Denmark is in the lead, followed closely by the Netherlands, while Belgium and Italy lag behind. After the discussion on mortgage take-up (Section 3.2), these results are not surprising. However, the translation of outstanding mortgages to net expected costs is not simply a linear transformation.

Institutions, homeowners and mortgage contracts differ, all affecting the actual costs (and risks) that a mortgage implies for the individual borrower. The ratio of mortgage take-up to the net costs-equivalent varies from 1.10 in the Netherlands to 1.37 in Belgium and France. The costs are relatively high in Belgium and France, given the preference for more traditional mortgages (serial/annuity, short duration, and long fixed-interest periods). Modern mortgages and a favourable mortgage interest tax relief system lead to a low level of expected costs for Dutch homeowners. As always, however, low costs come with a disadvantage: more risks.

The uncertainty regarding future costs is somewhat low for traditional mortgages; certainly if combined with long fixed-interest periods, which eliminate all interest rate risks. This can be clearly illustrated by comparing the risks (semi-variance) over the six countries. The risks in the UK are especially high due to preferences for the riskier/more uncertain mortgage types and short fixed-interest periods. Naturally, these risks also depend on actual mortgage take-up.

Secondly, the risk of mortgages can be dealt with in terms of default and repossession risks, which are also shown in Table 5.2. Only in France, the

Table 5.2 Costs and implied risk of actual mortgage take-up (recent buyers, EU6, 2003)

	Belgium	Denmark	France	Italy	Netherlands	UK
Costs (€)						
Mean	95,549	228,566	144,061	81,582	214,767	164,324
Trimmed mean	95,577	228,718	144,106	81,553	214,957	163,215
Minimum	86,129	216,422	136,021	78,108	133,526	130,105
Maximum	102,991	233,558	150,453	86,170	250,116	224,113
90%-percentile	98,519	230,670	146,765	83,215	227,888	195,053
Risks (€)						
Standard-deviation	2,420	2,218	2,202	1,238	10,499	20,062
Semi-variance	1,667	1,148	1,489	922	7,062	15,952
Arrears (%, annualised)	--	0.11	2.21	0.56	2.92	3.79
Repossession (%, annualised)	--	0.01	0.34	0.01	1.42	3.26
Negative equity (€)	--	--	--	--	-15.47*	--
Initial mortgage take-up (€)	69,291	182,937	104,439	65,352	194,982	123,642

Source: see Table 4.2

* The average negative equity when a household is repossessed (or 'voluntary' forced to move) amounts up to ~€ 13,500.

Netherlands and the UK are these risks significant[48]. These results partly reflect differences in mortgage take-up and partly the higher volatility in income in these countries. The probability that arrears will end in repossession is even smaller (repossession may be compulsory or voluntary, see Section 4.4). Here, legislation and regulation also play an important role; in some countries, such as France, where strong consumer protection laws lead to long foreclosure procedures, the probability is virtually non-existent (the opposite applies in the UK). Finally, the probability of negative equity – occurring only when house prices fall below the outstanding mortgage at the time of repossession – is more or less negligible[49], except in the Netherlands. This stems, of course, from the definition of negative equity, i.e. conditional on repossession, house price volatility and the net outstanding mortgages.

The default and repossession risks shown in Table 5.2 are annualised percentages. In reality, both risks show a distinct pattern over time: High in the first years[50] after taken out the mortgage and then rapidly declining thereafter, when positive income changes and repaying the initial debt diminish the probability of any payment problems. As example, in Figure 5.3 the default and repossession probabilities over time for the Netherlands are shown; again for the paradigmatic case representing the average recent buyer.

---

48 Note again, that these figures relate to recent buyers only. Data on arrears as presented in Table 3.7 refers to all borrowers/buyers; hence considerably lower than in Table 5.2.

49 Risk indicators are not necessarily proportional to the initial mortgage take-up.

50 Lending criteria of financial institutions will prevent arrears occurring within the first years.

Figure 5.3 Default and repossession probability by year (The Netherlands)

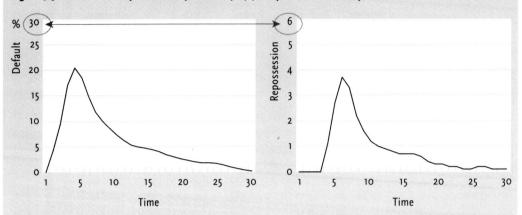

Default rates represent the percentage of households experiencing mortgage costs as a heavy burden leading to arrears of more than 1 month. Repossession rates indicate the unsustainability of the housing costs leading to repossession or voluntarily move from the property.

Costs[51] and risks of all available mortgages

Next, Figure 5.4 depicts the costs and risks of all available mortgage contracts, i.e. the costs and risks of each of the 30 combinations defined in Table 5.2. Only the mortgage contract specifications were altered in the analysis, not the characteristics of the individual borrower or the amount actually taken up. Note that in some countries, see discussion in Chapter 3, not all mortgage types are available or that borrowers' accessibility is hampered (Section 3.5). Obviously, these mortgage supply restrictions limit the range of the options available to the borrower. However, for the derivation of the implied risk attitude of borrowers the lack of options is not important. Of course, choice behaviour of borrowers is not influenced by the set of mortgage contract options outside their scope.

The first and foremost conclusion to derive from Figure 5.4 is that actual mortgage take-up of recent buyers can be considered rational and optimal; i.e. the chosen option constitute a cost/risk trade-off on or near the efficiency frontier. Next, although the pattern of costs and risks diverges for the different mortgages between countries, some general conclusions can still be drawn. One might expect investment mortgages, with their additional uncertainty about share price developments, and mortgages with more variable interest rates to bring more risks than other mortgage types, but this does not always hold true: it actually depends on both the institutional context and the economic cycle. So for instance, if long-term inflation is higher (e.g. the UK[52]), variable interest rates lead to lower costs and lower risks in the end. Similarly, if the correlation between interest rates and share prices is negative (again, in the UK) the mix of variable interest and investment can be profitable, particu-

---

51 These costs include the capitalised risk in case of arrear and repossession.

52 See also mortgage take-up in the past in Italy; given the high inflation, half the borrowers opted for variable interest rates.

Figure 5.4 Costs and risks of different mortgage products (EU6, x €1,000)

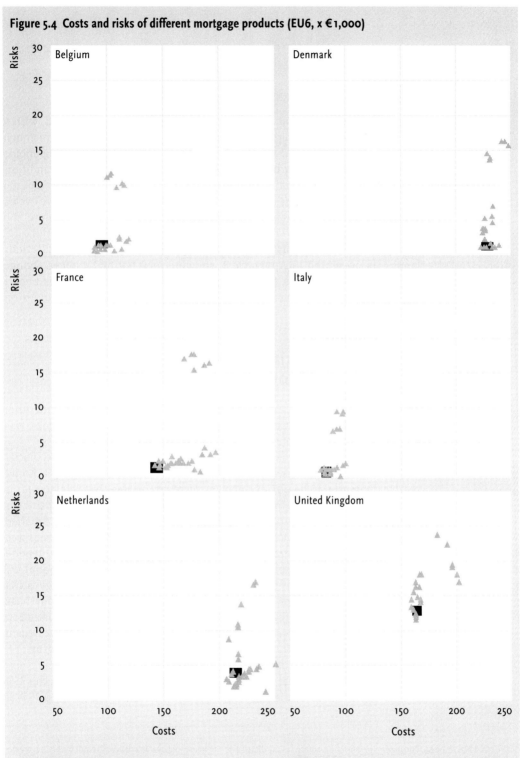

Vertical axis: risk (semi-variance); horizontal axis: expected costs; ■ actual choice, i.e. a weighted average of the different mortgages chosen in a specific country.

larly if the mortgage period is modest. In Belgium, on the other hand, with a tax system that favours repayment, serial and annuity mortgages are much less costly, particularly if the mortgage period is relatively short. Households in Belgium would be even better off if they were to abandon their traditional preference for long-term fixed-interest periods. Other countries, of course, have their own characteristics when it comes to institutions, economic cycles, borrowers, and factors that affect the optimal mortgage choice. Therefore, the trade-off between (higher) costs and (added) risks differs in each case.

Finally, a partial analysis – here exclusively for recent buyers in the Netherlands – is presented in Appendix B, showing how optimal choices change under different conditions (see also Neuteboom, 2005). This analysis shows along other lines the way in which institutions may shape the outcomes on the mortgage market.

5.4 Risk attitudes of borrowers in a cross-country framework

Before presenting and discussing the risk attitudes of recent buyers and other groups, a few words need to be said about the relationship between risks, risk attitudes and mortgage take-up.

Many treat mortgage take-up as synonymous with risks (see the discussion in Chapter 1), but does the actual mortgage debt taken up by a homeowner really matter? The obvious answer seems to be 'yes', but this answer is certainly not always true. In fact, it is more wrong than right. Recall the discussion on the concept of risk and risk attitude in Chapter 2, which finished off with the statement that risk is a combination of hazards, probabilities and impact (consequences). Obviously, neither hazards nor probabilities depend on actual mortgage take-up. The consequences do; but households adopt different strategies to prevent them. The first and most plausible strategy is not to borrow to their limits; for some, this means either postponing the purchase of a house altogether or accepting one of lesser quality. By way of illustration, see Figure 5.5, which shows the maximum borrowing capacity[53] for recent buyers and first-time buyers in comparison with actual mortgage take-up.

Although differences exist across the countries, it is clear that recent buyers mostly do not go for the maximum. Generally, they remain below the 75% mark; i.e. their actual loan is in percentage of actual mortgage take-up 75% or

---

[53] The maximum borrowing capacity is calculated with the household characteristics of recent buyers (income), the prevailing system of housing provision, mortgage interest rates, typical mortgage characteristics and, finally, the credit constraints (maximum debt service ratio allowed).

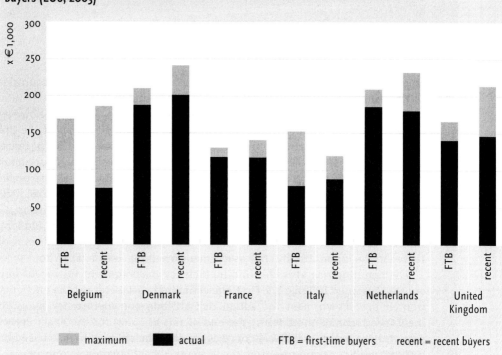

Figure 5.5 Actual mortgage take-up and maximum borrowing capacity, for recent buyers and first-time buyers (EU6, 2003)

maximum   actual   FTB = first-time buyers   recent = recent buyers

Maximum borrowing capacity for recent buyers is excluding the freefall of housing equity embedded in the 'old' house.

less. Here, Belgium homeowners being the most cautious, using, on average, slightly less than 40% of the maximum borrowing capacity; buying a relative cheap house is the main contributor, family loans and/or personal savings make up the difference. This lending behaviour effectively creates a buffer for a drop of 25% in household income or a rise of one third in the housing costs (when actual borrowing is restricted to 75% of the maximum). Over time, when the income increases and the outstanding mortgage debt decreases[54] these margins improve further. The average buyer, however, is not credit constraint; i.e. he is not necessarily a short-term cost minimiser but his utility depends on minimising both costs and risks.

The results (Figure 5.5) show that first-time buyers differ (slightly) from other recent buyers (lending less, but actual take-up is closer to their maximum borrowing capacity!); although it is fair to say that lenders assessment procedures play the more decisive role here. Since lenders focus with this group primarily on the loan-to-value ratio, low loan-to-income ratios for first-time buyers indicate that the credit-constraints are more based on lack of necessary savings (i.e. initial down payment) than on household income.

Risk attitudes, the core issue of this thesis, do not depend directly on the

---

54 Actually, this rate depends on the chosen mortgage contract.

amount of outstanding mortgage debt either. Households in some countries do borrow substantially more than in others in terms of loan-to-income ratio – which will increase the potential negative consequences for them. However, the argument here is that these outcomes are merely a reflection of the prevailing conditions on the national housing market (house price level, rental market, quality, locational aspects, etcetera), and are not a sign of greater housing consumption whilst accepting higher risks[55]. Risk attitudes, i.e. the preference of borrowers for mortgage products with relatively lower or higher risks, depend solely on the choice from the range of available mortgage contracts, all of which are within the means of the borrower. Naturally, in the short and long run, the risk profile differs for the various mortgage contracts, but this is capitalised in the initial cost and risk assessment when the loan is taken out.

The resulting risk attitudes and inefficiency measurement for recent buyers are presented in Table 5.3. First, the estimated parameters of the efficiency frontier are shown, next the actual risk attitude and inefficiency measurement (see technical note 5.2 at the end of this chapter) for the exact derivation of these indicators). Recall, once again, that the analysis here is based on a paradigmatic case representing the 'average' recent buyer in a country.

The following conclusions may be drawn from the results reported in Table 5.3:

- Recent buyers in all countries are risk-averse, i.e. the coefficient is between −1 and 0. Hence, they choose options with relatively low risks and high-expected costs.
- With the exception of borrowers in the UK, the differences between countries (for recent buyers) are small. Households in the UK do opt for more risk-inclined mortgages, but still even, they are risk averse.
- In most countries, the inefficiency indicator is rather low, indicating that households (recent buyers) make the optimal choice (behave rationally), i.e. they choose an option on the efficiency frontier, given their personal background and current institutional context. Of course, the range of mortgage products on offer on the market also influences the optimal mortgage. If, like in for instance France and Italy, the options are for most households limited and did not alter over time, the efficiency of the choice is secured.
- At first glance, households in the Netherlands and the UK seem to have relatively high inefficiency measurements (6.2288 and 4.8107 respectively), i.e. they could choose an option closer to the efficiency frontier (than the one actually chosen). The potential benefits – which constitute up to €4,404 (NL) and €3,402 (UK) in terms of lower costs and risks over the full duration of the mortgage –, are relativity small compared to the initial out-

---

55 In fact, there is no hard evidence that households in high-lending countries consume more housing services (in terms of size, dwelling type, etc.) than elsewhere in Europe.

Table 5.3 Risk attitudes and rational choice behaviour of recent buyers (EU6, 2003)

	Belgium	Denmark	France	Italy	Netherlands	UK
Efficiency frontier ($y = \alpha e^{\beta x}$)						
α	5.3800	5,846.2000	14.5200	88.9600	198.2900	1,192.5000
β	-0.0195	-0.0365	-0.0140	-0.0568	-0.0205	-0.0283
Risk attitude	-0.0196	-0.0504	-0.0287	-0.0498	-0.0547	-0.3555
Inefficiency measurement	1.1569	0.3287	0.6102	0.0777	6.2288	4.8107

The risk attitude is always below zero, given the negative trade-off between lower risk and higher expected costs. If the risk attitude is equal to -1, the decision-maker (borrower) is considered risk-neutral; if the risk attitude is between -1 and 0, he is considered risk-averse. Finally, if the risk attitude is lower than -1, he is considered a risk-seeker. The inefficiency frontier, an indicator of rational behaviour, is proportional to initial mortgage take-up.

standing mortgage debt[56]. Note also that the huge, and increasing, number of products households in these countries may choose from, made it increasingly difficult for households to make a well-informed decision (i.e. information and search costs are high!).

The focus in the remainder of this section will be on the differences and similarities in risk attitude in different household categories. Figure 5.6 shows the results for three different groups of households, based on age, income and housing market position. The ranking between countries, as shown in Table 5.4, does not change if the focus shifts to different household categories. Nevertheless, some general conclusions can be drawn (here recent buyers are used as a benchmark):

- All households are risk-averse, even when focusing on the different groups. Borrowers in the UK are in the lead, but even they can be considered risk-averse.
- If house prices and volatility in house prices are higher – e.g. the Netherlands and the UK – first-time buyers have to accept a higher risk in order succeeding on the homeownership market. In general, the 'all borrowers'-group is slightly more risk-averse than recent buyers are. Given their profile (see Chapter 3), this outcome is not unexpected.
- Low-income buyers (1st quintile) across Europe tend to be more risk-averse than others are. Given their income level and lack of resources to overcome any temporary financial problem, this is only to be expected. However, Danish and Dutch borrowers with a lower income accept relatively more risks. The prospects of home equity, fuelled by recent house price increases, in combination with a good safety net if things go wrong, prompt them to take on higher risks[57]. Conversely, high(er)-income households (3rd quintile) have average risk attitudes, with the exception of the UK[58].

---

56 Note also that in these countries the number of mortgage products is high and still increasing, meaning that it is not always feasible for individual customers to make the optimal mortgage choice.

57 I.e. they consider homeownership as less risky than other groups (Turner *et al.*, 2006); a notion that is not necessarily valid.

58 In the UK, households in the fourth quintile, push up the average.

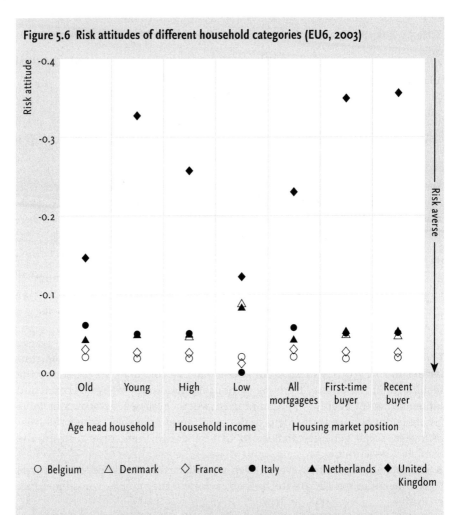

Figure 5.6 Risk attitudes of different household categories (EU6, 2003)

This figure shows the calculated risk attitude for divers groups of households based on age (old = > 55+; young = < 30), income (high 3rd quintile; low 1st quintile) and housing market position (all borrowers, first-time buyers and recent buyers (= benchmark)).

■ Younger households (< 30 years), mostly first-time buyers, are willing to accept higher costs and risks to succeed on the housing market, although the differences, with the exception of UK households, are not high. On the other hand, older households, with a profile comparable with all borrowers are more risk-averse. So apparently, younger cohorts have different risk attitudes than older cohorts[59].

■ Finally, although not shown in Figure 5.5, the inefficiency measurement for the different household categories indicates, as expected, that the more time has passed since choosing the mortgage, the greater the inefficiency, thereby indicating that transaction and search costs are relatively high and that borrowers do not attempt to optimise their mortgage immediately. On the other

---

59 However, it is not always easy to disentangle choice behaviour from 'forced shopping'.

hand, the absolute benefit the average household potentially can acquire is very limited (see the discussion on the risk attitudes of recent buyers).

5.5 Conclusions

In general, the households in the sample choose rational; i.e. they choose a mortgage that constitutes both the lowest costs and risks. At the same time, the typical mortgage contract specifications – in terms of mortgage type, duration, fixed interest rate period etc. – differs across countries. These, at first sight, contrasting results highlight the importance of both the institutional context and the differences in households' characteristics in shaping the optimal mortgage contract for households. Next, all recent buyers in the different countries express a risk-averse attitude towards mortgages, as one may expect given the high financial commitment at stake. Zooming in on different household categories – by age, income or housing market position – did not alter this view.

Thus, given the results of the analysis, what can we conclude with respect to the hypotheses formulated in Chapter 1:

I. *Households behave rational when choosing a specific mortgage type; i.e. they choose a mortgage that constitute, for them, the lowest costs and/or risks.*

II. *The risk attitude of owner-occupiers with similar individual characteristics is identical across countries when adjusted for differences in institutions and the structure of national mortgage markets.*

The results presented earlier in this chapter confirmed the first hypothesis. I.e. the inefficiency measurement is close to zero ($z \approx 0$) for all countries. Households do choose optimal, given their personal (socio-economic) circumstances, the institutional context and the structure of the national mortgage market. I.e. the implicit assumption of rational behaviour seems to be valid.

Two versions of the second hypothesis were discussed. In the weak version of the hypothesis, the expectation was that all households in the different countries are revealing a risk-averse attitude towards mortgages; while in the strong version of the hypothesis no significant differences in the risk attitude of owner-occupiers with similar individual characteristics exist between countries, i.e.

$$H_{0,weak} \quad : \quad \forall_{countries\ a..n} \quad F'(x)_{country} < 0$$
$$H_{0,strong} \quad : \quad \forall_{countries\ a..n} \quad F'(x)_{country=a} = ... = F'(x)_{country=n} < 0$$

In Table 5.4, the risk attitudes for different categories are presented, including some test statistics showing whether the outcome in one country is significantly different from the median. A sign test, based on the median is here

Table 5.4 Testing the hypothesis: risk attitudes of borrowers across countries and household categories

	Housing market position			Income		Age	
	Recent buyer	First-time buyer	All borrowers	Low	High	Young	Old
Belgium	-0.0196	-0.0199	-0.0212	-0.0195	-0.0196	-0.0199	-0.0206
Denmark	-0.0503	-0.0539	-0.0451	-0.0934	-0.0498	-0.0532	-0.0463
France	-0.0287	-0.0287	-0.0320	-0.0157	-0.0289	-0.0286	-0.0322
Italy	-0.0498	-0.0498	-0.0576	-0.0007	-0.0498	-0.0495	-0.0599
Netherlands	-0.0547	-0.0555	-0.0440	-0.0859	-0.0521	-0.0524	-0.0447
UK	-0.3554	-0.3500	-0.2302	-0.1231	-0.2578	-0.3261	-0.1487
Median	-0.0501	-0.0519	-0.0446	-0.0527	-0.0498	-0.0510	-0.0455
Median-test 95%-confidence interval							
Lower	-0.1858	-0.1850	-0.1272	-0.1059	-0.1442	-0.1741	-0.0939
Upper	0.0856	0.0812	0.0379	0.0004	0.0445	0.0721	0.0028

This table shows risk attitudes by country and household category. To compare means a simple sign-test was performed; the lower and upper value of the 95%-confidence interval is shown at the bottom two rows. Dark shading indicates that the country/household categories' risk attitude is below the lower bound. See also the note on Figure 5.6.

more appropriate given the non normal distribution of the risk attitudes across countries (households in the UK seem to be outliers).

Clearly, in all countries, for all household categories – not just recent buyers – the risk attitude is between –1 and 0 indicating risk-averseness, so the weak hypothesis is confirmed. However, UK households in all categories exhibit significantly less risk-averseness than comparable household categories in other countries; the differences between households in the other five countries are insignificant. So, the stronger version of the hypothesis $H_{0,strong}$ must be rejected.

Further research will demonstrate whether these differences – between the UK and the other countries – are just temporal phenomena reflecting prevailing conditions or are more persistent showing different risk attitudes based on cultural traditions.

Technical notes to Chapter 5

Note 5.1 Derivation of the efficiency frontier

Suppose someone chooses option A, represented in the diagram below (Figure 5.7) by the midpoint of the intersecting lines.

An option is considered as (possibly) lying on the efficiency frontier if there are no alternatives in the southwest quadrant, marked 'Efficient options'. On the other hand, any option in the northeast quadrant is inefficient for a borrower, since there is at least one option available, mortgage choice A, which

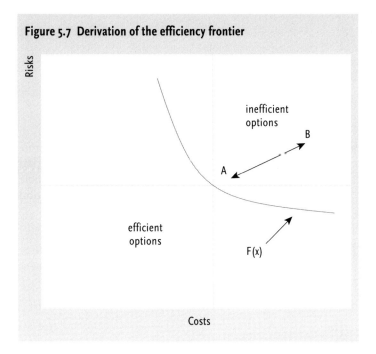

Figure 5.7 Derivation of the efficiency frontier

Risks

inefficient
options

B

A

efficient
options

F(x)

Costs

implies both lower costs and risks[60]. Hence, these options cannot be on the efficiency frontier either. Thirdly, it is not easy to assess whether any options in the southeast or northwest quadrant are on the efficiency frontier as this depends on the exact shape of the efficiency frontier.

Two steps are needed to establish the exact shape of the efficiency frontier $F(x)$:

- Possible points on the efficiency frontier are selected by applying two simple rules:
  1. Choose the options with minimum costs and minimum risks.
  2. Add to those any options that comply with: $\forall i = 1..30 \quad (c_i > \tilde{c} \vee r_i > \tilde{r})$ (i.e. no options in the southwest quadrant).
- The efficiency frontier is estimated based on this selected set and will have an exponential form of $F(x) = \alpha e^{\beta x}$, with $\beta < 0$.

Note 5.2 Derivation of risk attitude and inefficiency measurement
It has already been established that if someone chooses option A on the efficiency frontier $F(x)$, his choice is by definition optimal. The risk attitude shows us the trade-off between the risks and costs that a borrower is willing to accept: in other words, the increase in expected costs that someone is willing to pay in order to reduce the risk by one unit. The risk attitude is, in this case, equal to $F'(x)$, i.e. the slope of a line tangent to point A. Hence, given the shape of the relevant part of the efficiency frontier, the first derivative, the risk attitude equals: $F'(x) = \beta(\alpha+1)e^{\beta x}$. Risk attitudes are normally negative; a higher level – closer to zero – indicates more risk aversion.

---

60 This normative approach is based on a rational decision-maker and, implicitly, on a decision-maker with full knowledge and low transaction costs so that he can adjust his past choices quickly to changing circumstances.

If, for whatever reason, a borrower chooses an inefficient option B, or – more likely – his actual choice shifts over time to an inefficient sub-optimal position, the risk attitude is not readily calculable. If, however, we assume that the shape of the efficiency frontier has not changed over time[61], it is possible to transpose the chosen option to a point on $F(x)$, i.e. a linear transformation, so that $y_b-z=F(x_b-z)$. Then the risk attitude can be derived as $F'(x_b-z)$.

Finally, The proportion z can be used to measure the extent of the inefficiency, i.e. the distance between B and B' is by definition: $\sqrt{2z^2}$.

⎯⎯⎯⎯⎯⎯

61 This assumption implies that no fundamental break occurred in the institutional context, since the moment the individual household had chosen its mortgage.

⎯⎯⎯⎯⎯⎯

6 Facts, findings and conclusions

6.1 Summary

Homeownership in the Netherlands and elsewhere in Europe is increasingly popular and growing. As most (prospective) homeowners are unable to finance the purchase of their property from their own resources, one can expect an increase in mortgage take-up. Recent growth brought outstanding mortgage debt to an astonishing €5.1 trillion (EU15, 2005), representing over 40% of all outstanding bank credits and equal to more than one third of the joint GDP. Mortgage debt within Europe differs both on a macro and on a micro level.

This growing outstanding mortgage debt is a concern to the financial authorities, in both the Netherlands and elsewhere. Explicitly, a growing mortgage debt is seen a good indicator of the risks involved for households, the financial sector and the state. More implicitly, the pattern of mortgage take-up is considered symptomatic of the underlying risk attitude of homeowners and borrowers; hence, a high debt suggests a more risk-seeking attitude and vice-versa.

In this thesis, both notions are challenged. Mortgage risks are complex and multiple, depending on the institutional context and the characteristics of the borrowers and mortgage contracts. Taking out a mortgage is also a long-term financial commitment for a household. Circumstances can, and do, alter over time (e.g. interest rates, income, house prices, inflation) and influence both the expected costs and risks.

This thesis was organised along five research questions (Chapter 1). I will present the remainder of this summary with reference to those questions.

Research question 1 – How, and to what extent, does mortgage take-up vary in Europe, and to what extent does the relevant context within Europe diverge?
As it turns out, it is not easy to sketch a clear picture, let alone a ranking-order of the different countries, based on mortgage take-up, institutional differences and similarities, characteristics of (prospective) homeowners and national mortgage markets. In terms of mortgage take-up it was indeed possible to categorise high debt countries (Denmark, the Netherlands and the UK) and low debt countries (Belgium, France, Italy), both on a macro and micro level. In terms of institutional differences, characteristics of borrowers and the typical mortgage contracts on offer, no clear picture emerged. Countries do all have their own set of long standing institutions – like the much-quoted mortgage interest tax relief, but also a wide range of other issues, such as consumer protection regulation (e.g. procedures surrounding repossessions) and the level of social security (unemployment benefit, pensions, etc.) – shaping both demand and supply on national mortgage markets. Some evidence on convergence was found, but national differences are well grounded in policies, laws, and public opinion. Their partial effects were found to be both substantive as different across the EU6; their implications in terms of costs and

risks for individual homeowners remain obscure. These issues were more extensively discussed in Chapter 3.

Research question 2 – How can the expected costs and risks of a mortgage be quantified for an owner-occupier?
Given the multiple nature of the risks and the dynamics involved, transforming mortgage take-up into the costs and risks of mortgages for owner-occupiers is a complicated affair; all the more so in a cross-country framework. Without a common denominator, it would be impossible to identify, compare (or resolve) different risks. Therefore, if we are to draw any conclusions on the risks that homeowners are apparently willing to take, we should not concentrate on mortgage take-up itself but on the net costs and risks it represents to the borrower.

Actual costs and risks are time depending (up to 30 years). In order to cope with that, in this thesis a stochastic model was built in which the determining factors (e.g. income, interest rates) and the institutional context, mortgage market and household characteristics were combined to calculate expected costs and risks (including default, repossession and negative equity risk). These issues were more extensively discussed in Chapter 4.

Research question 3 – How can this framework be extended to compare the risk attitude of borrowers across countries?
That model was then extended to assess the risk attitude of a borrower. Recapping on the discussion in Chapter 2 on the derivation of the risk attitude from actual behaviour, we need to be clear that it is not so much the stated attitude that matters, but primarily the revealed attitude based on actual choice-behaviour. The idea was to ascertain the attitude of borrowers by comparing their chosen option (i.e. mortgage contracts) in terms of costs and risks, hence incorporating the effect of institutions and different household and mortgage characteristics, with all alternative options on the market. This will make it possible to evaluate whether the chosen mortgage contract is optimal and to ascertain how far the borrower chooses an option with a low or high-risk profile. These issues were more extensively discussed in Chapter 4.

Research question 4 – Do households, on average, choose the optimal mortgage, i.e. act rationally?
Research question 5 – To what extent does the risk attitude of homogeneous groups of owner-occupiers differ between countries within Europe?
The results show that the cost-and-risk equivalents of mortgages differ substantially across Europe (EU6), potentially mounting to a 34% difference between low-cost and high-cost countries. Not surprisingly, the results also indicate that, given the institutional context and the characteristics of borrowers, the optimal mortgage contract differs across countries. For instance, in the Netherlands an interest-only mortgage is less risky than a serial loan, while

the opposite is true in Belgium.

Nevertheless, households do make – more or less – an optimal choice and opt for the mortgage contracts with the lowest costs and risks trade-off. Households do choose rational, given their personal (socio-economic) circumstances, the institutional context and the structure of the national mortgage market. Therefore, differences in outcome across countries are not an indicator of different behaviour of borrowers.

In terms of risk attitude, the analysis showed that borrowers in all counties are risk-averse. However, households in the UK seem to accept more risks than households in other countries, but even they still behave in a risk-averse manner. Further analysis for different groups in a country (e.g. first-time buyers, low-income households) did not reveal wide deviations from this pattern.

Both research questions 4 and 5 were more extensively discussed in Chapter 5.

6.2 Discussion of findings

This section deals with two issues. First, the return to the hypothesis: did the research confirm or reject the hypothesis? Second, how do the results from this study relate to findings from other projects and perspectives?

Testing the hypotheses
This study started with the following two hypotheses (Chapter 1):
I. *Households behave rational when choosing a specific mortgage type; i.e. they choose a mortgage that constitute, for them, the lowest costs and/or risks.*
II. *The risk attitude of owner-occupiers with similar individual characteristics is identical across countries when adjusted for differences in institutions and the structure of national mortgage markets.*

Both hypotheses were confirmed. Households do act rationally (the inefficiency measurement is close to zero). Therefore, one may conclude that rational choice theory – though often attacked on grounds of unrealism in actual decision-making behaviour of households – holds, when applied to the risk attitudes of borrowers. The weak version of the second hypothesis – i.e. all households in the different countries are revealing a risk-averse attitude towards mortgages – was confirmed as well. However, the strong version of the hypothesis – no significant differences in the risk attitude of owner-occupiers with similar individual characteristics exist between countries – needs to be rejected. Specifically households in the UK turned out to be less risk averse than those in other countries.

Hence, different outcomes in mortgage take-up across Europe do not necessarily reflect differences in risk attitude, but merely differences in the underlying institutional context, household characteristics and the available mortgage contracts. This thesis highlighted the important role these factors play in shaping the optimal mortgage choice for individual borrowers across Europe.

The starting point of this study was the observation that many – financial authorities, policy-makers and academics alike – interpret cross-country differences in mortgage take-up as indications of differences in the underlying risk behaviour of individual households. There are two problems with linking macro indicators on mortgage take-up with the underlying risk attitudes; one is empirical, the other conceptual.

The empirical issue has been dealt with above. The conceptual problem is well known as the ecological fallacy, i.e. interpreting aggregated data on an individual level. The analysis of this thesis reveals that formulating conclusions on household behaviour by analysing the data on a cross-country level does not hold either. In other words, the analysis showed that the correlation between mortgage take-up on a macro level and the underlying risk attitudes is rather weak. Careful quantification on a micro level is needed to identify the true risk attitudes of borrowers; not because such an analysis (re)discovered unknown or neglected hazards (= origins of risks), but because the probability of these hazards and the consequences are hard to assess if not quantified. Explicit quantification, as performed in this thesis, leads to more objective and hence more transparent results. More generally, there is still a need to shift the focus of international comparative research from descriptive analysis with some basic macro indicators added, to a higher level: i.e. *"to quantify the features of national systems in a consistent fashion"* (Oxley, 2001). More cross-country studies on a micro level are needed to improve our understanding of (national) housing systems.

Confronting the constructivist approach

The risk attitudes (of mortgagees) can be analysed in different ways. In Chapter 2, two different strands of research were discussed: the realist versus the constructivist approach (Jasonoff, 1998). Although, this thesis followed the realist approach, which implicitly assumes that all risks are quantifiable and that rational decision-makers decide accordingly, it would be of interest to see how these results hold to a constructivist approach.

The constructivists approach, with its emphasis on stated risk perceptions[62] is within the context of mortgage decision making a relatively new research area. Recent research brought in some interesting observations (e.g. OSIS project, see Horsewood and Neuteboom, 2006 and Elsinga et al., 2007[63] for an overview).

---

62 One problem with stated preferences is, of course, the ex-post rationalisation of initial decision making.

63 These research results were partly based on in dept interviews amongst homeowners and renters in eight countries. These interviews focused on household perceptions' of security and insecurity.

Firstly, the risk awareness of households is rather low, i.e. many people are unaware of the (many) risks of homeownership: "*Overall, most respondents recognised few risks to their housing when first asked the question. … homeowners did not perceive many housing related risks*" (Quilgars and Jones, 2007, p. 279) and "*Interviewees were asked what risks might affect their housing situation. It was striking that people were initially unsure as to how to answer this question*" (Toussaint and Elsinga, 2007a, p. 190). Secondly, most households are quite positive about the future, i.e. their risk perception is rather low: "*.. risks were perceived as unlikely to happen; moreover, people trusted their capabilities and resources to solve problems if they showed up*" (Toussaint and Elsinga, 2007b, p. 289). Moreover, when things would take a turn for the worse, many people – rightfully or wrongly – rely on family support and social institutions to help them when necessary. Respondents in countries like Belgium and the Netherlands commonly mentioned reliance on social security; while households in Portugal and the UK were not quite as sure about the role of national government, and relied more on family support respectively self-management. Thirdly, across Europe, households perceive homeownership as an important aspect of life. Most households receive a sense of security of owning their own property; both in financial terms (when repaid, low housing costs remain) and for more ontological reasons. In that respect, households do not want to risk their home with financial (mortgage) products regarded, by them, as "risky".

Therefore, these results do not appear to contradict the main conclusion of the thesis: borrowers across Europe are mostly risk-averse, irrespective of age, income or household type (not withstanding the fact that many households do not assess their risk adequately!).

Then, buying a home and certainly mastering the financial details prove for many households across Europe a difficult task. That is, understanding the uncertainties involved and assessing them accurately is a necessity well beyond the potential for many. On the other hand, it is no longer realistic in our complex modern society to expect each individual to have adequate knowledge of every kind of risk let alone how to address them. *How do households deal with this apparent lack of decision-making capabilities?* Reliance on tradition, family advice, and the opinions of experts, often intermediaries with their own interests to serve, is frequently the chosen way out. Individual households get their information from dealing directly with professionals; but, more importantly, their perceptions are twisted by the popular media. However, the impact on individual risk perception is two fold. The discourse between the different agents – communicated by the press, inducing government to alter institutions – influences not only the awareness and understanding of the risks involved for individuals[64] but reaching to them the

---

64 Nevertheless, the knowledge of risks involved remains imperfect (see discussion in Elsinga *et al.*, 2007).

optimal solution as well. I.e. this channel of communication is used – some will say misused – by different stakeholders to promote public or private solutions to these risks (e.g. mortgage types, insurances etc.). The outcome of this process implies that households will show rational behaviour although their stated awareness and perceptions are far from perfect.

6.3 Implications

The results of the analysis show that, despite large differences in mortgage take-up, households across Europe are mainly risk-averse. Given the differences in the institutional context, the characteristics of both households and mortgage contracts, the costs and risks (consequences) of the same mortgage (type and amount) vary across countries. Hence, the optimal mortgage will not be identical in each country. One obvious policy-question arise from these results: *if mortgage take-up translates differently in terms of costs and risks on a micro level, what does this imply on a more aggregated level?*

Earlier, I mentioned that financial authorities across Europe are worried about the risks of high mortgage take-up not only for individual households but also for the financial sector and national governments. Their concerns stem primarily from the recent huge increase in mortgage take-up, resulting in high outstanding mortgage debts as a percentage of GDP. This data is replicated in Figure 6.1. It is clear that mortgage take-up in Denmark, the Netherlands and the UK is considerably higher than elsewhere[65]. However, how does this relate to the risks? Figure 6.1 presents as well, the cost-and-risk equivalent of the outstanding mortgage debt. These latter figures are calculated by estimating the costs and risks of the (mix of) mortgage types chosen by borrowers in a particular country and divided by the net household income of borrowers[66] (see Chapter 4 for more details). The final result, i.e. the cost-and-risk equivalent, is the weighted average of costs and risks of non-movers, recent buyers and first-time buyers.

It is obvious from Figure 6.1 that the cost-and-risk equivalent of outstanding mortgage debt grasps a different picture. The cost-and-risk equivalent for France and Italy is considerably higher, closing in on Denmark and the Netherlands and surpassing the UK with Belgium still trailing behind. This result stems from three factors. First, given the typical mortgage choice and the 'basic' system of housing provision in these countries, the costs and risks of a

─────────

65 The data shown is from 2003; meanwhile in 2006 the gap between high and low lending countries has increased (Italy 13% cf. the Netherlands 111% of GDP).

66 Taking into account households characteristics of the borrowers, the institutional context, and, of course, the exact amount borrowers has taken out.

─────────

Figure 6.1 Risk equivalents of outstanding mortgages, by country (normalised values 2003)

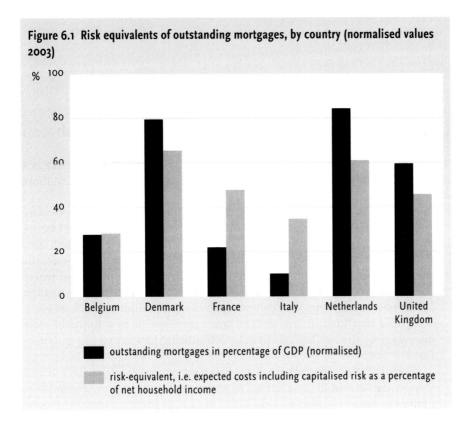

outstanding mortgages in percentage of GDP (normalised)

risk-equivalent, i.e. expected costs including capitalised risk as a percentage of net household income

mortgage are higher in France (24%) and Italy (14%) than in the Netherlands (= benchmark). Next, the net household income of borrowers in these countries is lower than in the Netherlands. Finally, there is a difference in the number of households (borrowers) that are obliged to pay for the outstanding mortgage.

Of course, a rise in mortgage take-up increases the risks for individuals, the financial sector and society in all countries, but the translation of mortgage debt to the cost-and-risk equivalent is not identical across Europe. Any increase in countries like France and Italy would constitute more risks than elsewhere, not least because the institutional context in the former countries is not geared to high mortgage take-up (e.g. repossession procedure, financial support for households in distress) while the repayment discipline of borrowers is less persistent (see, for instance, the high level of arrears).

The recent, rapid increase in outstanding mortgage debt in countries like France and Italy is creating greater risks there, than in Northwest Europe, i.e. the financial system in the Netherlands and the UK is more robust and efficient than elsewhere. Therefore, the focus of the debate on the risk of mortgages should be shifted southwards[67].

67 Though a comparison of the US and Europe was beyond the scope of this thesis, the results do show that risks for individual households and the economy can not be captured by some simple macro indicators alone. High-ranking countries based on loan-to-value and/or loan-to-income ratios (e.g. Denmark and the Netherlands) have low comparable cost-risk equivalents than other countries. Hence, worries about European housing and mortgage markets based on a comparison of e.g. loan-to-value ratios across the Atlantic are misleading.

6.4 Recommendations for further research

The results of this thesis and the discussion earlier in this chapter suggest some interesting lines of research. I shall elaborate on three of them in more detail:

1. *Risk mitigation on mortgage markets: the role of institutions.* Under pressure of for instance the ongoing globalisation, the traditional triangle of home-ownership, labour markets and social security is redefined. This will obviously lead to a different risk distribution between the financial sector, the state and households. In this process, (prospective) individual homeowners seem to be loosing ground. Therefore, there seems to be a growing need to invent new institutions that can mitigate the risk for individual homeowners. These new institutions are not synonymous with new forms of state intervention; the market can help by introducing new mortgage and/or insurance products.

   Nowadays, different solutions are being introduced (or discussed) across Europe, consisting of new forms of state provision, improved consumer rights etcetera. This thesis showed the impact of institutions on the costs and risks of mortgages. However, the analysis also showed that what works well in one country is not necessarily the best solution for another. We therefore need to extend our knowledge on the relationship between institutions and mortgage risks and risk distribution.

   Policymakers and private actors will then have better insights on how to alter the existing set of institutions to cope with the rapidly changing environment and (prospective) homeowners will remain more at ease with their housing situation and financial commitments.

2. *The impact of institutions on shaping supply and demand.* Mortgage markets have grown rapidly in the Netherlands and elsewhere. Recent growth has brought the outstanding mortgage debt to a staggering €5.1 trillion (EMF, 2005), i.e. over 40% of all outstanding bank credits and equal to more than one third of the joint GDP. Mortgage markets are a matter of growing concern for financial authorities (economic instability) and policymakers (consumer protection), sparking all kinds of regulatory changes. The lenders' environment is changing continuously and at an accelerating pace.

   However, the response to the demands of regulatory bodies can conflict with customer orientation. This is an unwelcome trend, certainly in times when we put more trust on the market to find housing solutions for citizens. The role of institutions and policies in shaping the demand for mortgages has been well-researched, institutional change will alter the optimal mortgage choices for individual households and increased competition will force lenders to fill in any gaps swiftly. The influence, however, that institutions and government policy have on firm-level behaviour (i.e. product development) and performance (i.e. costs) is, yet, uncharted territory, but it is obvious that such relationships do exist.

3. *Development of tools to assist households in making more informed choices about their mortgages.* Now and in the near future, mortgage decisions will remain the most important financial decision that a household will make. However, while society demands more responsibility from homeowners and the financial sector is more than happy to supply solutions, homeowners are stuck with a growing choice of mortgage products without knowing the exact implications and risks. There is a pressing need for tools to assist households to make a (more) informed choice. Households do behave rationally and will do so in the future; but the lack of knowledge and the limited learning capabilities of the 'average' household contradict with the more complex mortgage products on offer now and in the future. I.e. their pursuit for rationality is reaching its borders. Here, a more multidisciplinary approach is needed with economists saying what and psychologists saying how to tell (prospective) homeowners about the risks of different mortgage options.

References

Adams, J., 1995, **Risk**, London (UCL-Press).

Ball, M., 2004, **RICS Review of European Housing Markets 2003**, London (Knight Frank).

Ball, M. and M. Grilli, 1997, **Housing Markets and Economic Convergence in the European Union**, London (The Royal Institution of Chartered Surveyors).

Bartlett, W. and G. Bramley (eds.), 1994, **European Housing Finance: single market or mosaic?**, Bristol (SAUS Publ.).

Beck, U., 1992, **Risk Society**, London (Sage publication).

BIS (Bank of International Settlements), 2006, **Housing Finance in the Global Financial Market**, CGFS working group report, no. 26, Basel (BIS).

Boelhouwer, P., M. Haffner, P. Neuteboom and P. de Vries, 2004, House Prices and Income Tax in the Netherlands: an international perspective, in: **Housing Studies (3)**, pp. 415-432.

Böheim, R. and M.P. Taylor, 2000, My home was my castle: evictions and repossessions in Britain, in: **Journal of Housing Economics 9** (3), pp. 287-319.

Bosvieux, J. and B. Vorms, 2003, France, in: Doling J.F. and J. Ford (eds.) **Globalisation and Homeownership: Experiences in eight member States of the EU**, pp. 80-102, Delft (Delft University Press).

Boyle, P., M. Broadie and P. Glasserman, 1997, Monte Carlo Methods for Security Pricing, in: **Journal of Economic Dynamics and Control 21** (8 & 9), pp. 1267-1321.

Breslaw, J., I. Irvine and A. Rahman, 1996, Instrument Choice: the demand for mortgages in Canada, in: **Journal of Urban Economics 39** (3), pp. 282-302.

Brookes, M., M. Dicks and M. Pradhan, 1994, An Empirical Model of Mortgage Arrears and Repossessions, in: **Economic Modelling 11** (2), pp. 134-144.

Cairns, H. and G. Price, **A Critical Review of the UK Mortgage Default Literature**, Glasgow (University of Glasgow) (unpublished paper).

Campbell, J.Y. and J. Cocco, 2003, **Household Risk Management and Optimal Mortgage Choice**, NBER working paper 9759, Cambridge (MA), (NBER).

Capozza, D.R., D. Kazarian and T.A. Thomson, 1998, The Conditional Probability of Mortgage Default, in: **Real Estate Economics 26** (3), pp. 359-389.

Chen, R. and T.L. Tyler Yang, 1995, The Relevance of Interest Rate Processes in Pricing Mortgage-Backed Securities, in: **Journal of Housing Research 60** (2), pp. 315-329.

CML (Council of Mortgage Lenders), 2005, **CML Repossession Risk Review**, London (CML).

Conijn, J., F. den Breejen, M. Elsinga and P. Neuteboom, 2004, **Government Guarantees in the Rented and Owner-occupier Sector: an international comparison**, Zoetermeer (WEW).

Cox, J.C., J.E. Ingersoll and S.A. Ross, 1985, A Theory of the Term Structure of Interest Rates, in: **Econometrica 53** (2), pp. 385-407.

Croft, J., 2001, "A risk" or "at risk?" Reconceptualising Housing Debt in a Risk Welfare Society, in: **Housing Studies 16** (6), pp. 737-753.

Dean, M., 1999, Risk, Calculable and Incalculable, in: Lupton, D. (ed.) **Risk and Social-cultural Theory: New Directions and Perspectives**, pp. 131-159, Cambridge (Cambridge University Press).

Diamond Jr., D.B. and M.J. Lea, 1992, Housing Finance in Developed Countries: an international comparison of efficiency, in: **Journal of Housing Research 3** (1), (whole issue).

Diaz-Serrano, L., 2005, Income Volatility and Residential Mortgage Delinquency across the EU, in: **Journal of Housing Economics 14** (3), pp. 153-177.

Dol, C. and P. Neuteboom, 2005, **Insecurity Aspects of Homeownership: a cross-country analysis**, Delft (www.osis.bham.ac.uk, accessed 07 November 2006).

Doling, J.F., 2006, **Homeownership in Europe: Limits to growth**, paper given at CECODHAS Colloquium, Brussels (www.osis.bham.ac.uk, accessed 07 November 2006).

Doling, J.F. and N.J. Horsewood, 2004, Repayment, Risk and European Homeowners: the Interplay of Housing Markets, Labour Markets, Financial Markets and Social Security, in: **Housing Studies 19** (3), pp. 433-446.

Doling, J.F. and J. Ford (eds.), 2003, **Globalisation and Homeownership: Experiences in eight member states of the EU**, Delft (Delft University Press).

Donner, C., 2000, **Housing Policies in the European Union: theory and practice**, Vienna (Christian Donner).

Douglas, M. and A. Wildavsky, 1982, **Risk and Culture**, Berkeley (University of California Press).

Dutta, J., J.A. Sefton and M.R. Weale, 2001, Income Distribution and Income Dynamics in the UK, in: **Journal of Applied Econometrics 16** (5), pp. 599-617.

Early, F., 2005, What influences Mortgage Product?, in: **Housing Finance (7)**, pp. 1-8.

Eftekhari, B., Ch.S. Pedersen and S.E. Satchell, 2000, On the Volatility of Measures of Financial Risk: an Investigation using Returns from European Markets, in: **European Journal of Finance 6** (1), pp. 18-38.

Elsinga, M. and C. Dol, 2003, **De Geschiedenis van de Hypotheekgarantie in Nederland** (in Dutch) NHG reeks deel 2, Zoetermeer (WEW).

ECB (European Central Bank), 2003, **Structural Factors in the EU Housing Markets**, Frankfurt (ECB).

EC (European Commission), 2007, **Mortgage Credit in the EU** (green paper), Brussels (EC).

EMF (European Mortgage Federation), 1997, **Owner-occupied Housing in the European Union, tax aid, subsidies and costs**, Brussels (EMF).

EMF (European Mortgage Federation), 2003a, 2005, **Hypostat**, Brussels (EMF).

EMF (European Mortgage Federation), 2003b, **The Protection of the Mortgage Borrower in the European Union**, Brussels (EMF).

Eurostat, 1996, **The European Community Household Panel (ECHP): Survey, Methodology and Implementation**, Luxembourg (EU).

Ewald, F., 1991, Insurance and Risk, in: Burchell, G., C. Gordon and P. Miller (eds.) **The Foucault Effect: Studies in Governmentality**, pp. 197-211, Hemel Hampstead (Harvester Wheatsheaf).

Figueira, C., J. Glen and J. Nellis, 2005, A Dynamic Analysis of Mortgage Arrears in the UK Housing Market, in: **Urban Studies 42** (10), pp. 1755-1769.

Fischoff, B., S. Lichtenstein, P. Slovic, S.L. Derby and R.L. Keeny, **Acceptable Risk**, New York (Cambridge University Press).

Ford, J. and R. Burrows, 1999, The costs of Unsustainable Homeownership in Britain, in: **Journal of Social Policy 28** (2), pp. 305-330.

Ford, J., R. Burrows and S. Nettleton, 2001, **Homeownership in a Risk Society; a Social Analysis of Mortgage Arrears and Possessions**, London (Routledge).

Greene, W.H., 1993, **Econometric Analysis**, New York (Prentice Hall).

Goldberg, L.G. and A.J. Heuson, 1992, Fixed versus Variable Rate Financing: the Influence of Borrower, Lender and Market Characteristics, in: **Journal of Financial Services Research 6** (1), pp. 49-60.

Hall, R.E., 1990, **The Rational Consumer: Theory and Evidence**, Cambridge (Mass.) (MIT Press).

Hamnett, C., 1999, **Winners and Losers, Homeownership in modern Britain**, London (UCL Press).

Horsewood, N.J. and P. Neuteboom (eds.), 2006, **The Social Limits to Growth: Security and Insecurity Aspects of Homeownership**, Amsterdam (IOS Press).

IMF (International Monetary Fund), 2008, **World Economic Outlook: Housing and the Business Cycle**, Washington (IMF).

Jackson, J. and D. Kasterman, 1980, Default Risk on Home Mortgage Loans: a test of competing hypothesis, in: **Journal of Risk and Insurance 4** (3), pp. 678-690.

Jasanoff, S., 1998, The Political Science of Risk Perception, in: **Reliability Engineering and System Safety 59** (1), pp. 91-99.

Judge, G.G., R. Carter Hill, W. Griffiths, H. Lutkepohl and T.S. Lee, 1982, **Introduction to the Theory and Practice of Econometrics**, Chichester (John Wiley & Sons).

Kaplan, S. and B.J. Garrick, 1981, On the Quantitative Definition of Risk, in: **Risk Analysis 1** (1), pp. 11-27.

Kempson, E., S. McKay and M. Willitts, 2004, **Characteristics of Families in Debt and the Nature of Indebtedness** London (Department of Work and Pensions).

Kloth, M., 2004, **Payment Difficulties of Homeowners**, Cambridge, ENHR conference paper.

Lawson, J., 2005, **Homeownership and the 'Risk' Society: marginal home purchase in the Netherlands** (in Dutch), series no. 32, Utrecht (Nethur).

Leece, D., 2004, **Economics of the Mortgage Market, Perspectives on Household Decision Making**, Oxford (Blackwell Publishing).

Lupton, D., 1999, Introduction: Risk and Social-cultural Theory, in: Lupton, D. (ed.) **Risk and Social-cultural Theory: new directions and perspectives**, pp. 1-11, Cambridge (Cambridge University Press).

Maclennan, D., G. Meen, K. Gibb and M. Stephens, 1997, **Fixed Commitments, Uncertain Incomes: Sustainable Owner-occupation and the Economy**, York (Joseph Rowntree Foudation).

Maclennan, D., J. Muellbauer, and M. Stephens, 1999, **Asymmetries in Housing and Financial Market Institutions and EMU**, Centre for Economic Policy, discussion paper series no. 2062.

Markowitz, H., 1952, Portfolio Selection, in: **Journal of Finance 7** (1), pp. 77-91.

Marsumoto, M. and T. Nishimura, 1998, Mersenne Twister: A 623-Dimensionally Equidistributed.

Uniform pseudo-random number generator, in: **ACM Transactions on Modeling and Computer Simulation 8** (1), pp. 3-30.

Mercer Oliver Wyman, 2003, **Study on the Financial Integration of European Mortgage Markets**, Brussels (EMF).

Mercer Oliver Wyman and MITA, 2005, **Risk and Funding in European Residential Mortgages**, London (MWO/MITA).

Milevsky, M.A., 2001, **Mortgage Financing: Floating your Way to Prosperity**, IFID Research Centre, research report 01-01, Toronto (York University).

Mullainathen, S. and R.H. Thaler, 2000, **Behavioural Economics**, NBER working paper no. 7948, Cambridge (MA) (NBER).

Neftci, S.N., 2000, **An Introduction to the Mathematics of Financial Derivatives**, San Diego (Academic Press).

Neuteboom, P., 2008, Optimale Hypotheekkeuze van kopers, in: **Economisch Statistische Berichten 93** (4526), pp. 11-13.

Neuteboom, P., 2005, Optimal Mortgage Choices within different Institutional Contexts, in: Boelhouwer, P., J.F. Doling and M. Elsinga (eds.), **Homeownership, Getting in, Getting from, Getting out**, pp. 59-74, Delft (Delft University Press).

Neuteboom, P., 2004, A comparative Analysis of the Net Costs of a Mortgage for Homeowners in Europe, in: **Journal of Housing and the Built Environment 19** (2), pp. 169-186.

Neuteboom, P., 2003, A European Comparison of the Costs and Risks of Mortgages for Owner-occupiers, in: **European Journal of Housing Policy 3** (3), pp. 155-171.

Neuteboom, P., 2002, **Een Internationale Vergelijking van de Kosten en Risico's van Hypotheken** (in Dutch), series no. 19, Utrecht (Nethur).

Øksendal, B., 1992, **Stochastic Differential Equations**, Berlin (Springer-Verlag).

Oxley, M., 2001, Meaning, Science, Context and Confusion in Comparative Housing Research, in: **Journal of Housing and the Built Environment 16** (1), pp. 89-106.

Porter, T.M., 1995, **Trust in Numbers: the Pursuit of objectivity in science and public life**, Princeton (Princeton University Press).

Priemus, H., 1983, **Volkshuisvestingssysteem en Woningmarkt** (in Dutch), Volkshuisvesting in theorie en praktijk, Delft (Delft University Press).

Quilgars, D., A. Jones, 2007, United Kingdom: Safe as houses?, in Elsinga, M., P. de Decker, N. Teller and J. Toussaint (eds.), **Homeownership beyond Asset and Security: Perceptions of Housing related Security and Insecurity in eight European Countries**, pp. 259-286, Amsterdam (IOS Press).

Rebonato, R., 1998, **Interest-rate Option Models: Understanding, Analysing and Using models for Exotic Interest Rate Options,** Chichester (John Wiley & Sons).

Ross, S.M., 2002, **Simulation**, Florida (Academic Press).

Scanlon, K. and C. Whitehead, 2004, **International Trends in Housing Tenure and Mortgage Finance**, London (Council of Mortgage Lenders).

Scruggs, L. and J.P. Allan, 2003, **Trends in Welfare State: Decommodicifcation in Eighteen Advanced Industrial Democracies,** paper delivered at the annual meeting of the American Political Science Association.

Shiller, R.J., 1998, Human Behaviour and the Efficiency of the Financial System, in: Taylor, J.B. and M. Woodford (eds.) **Handbook of Macro-economics**, Amsterdam (Elsevier Science).

Steele, J.M., 2000, **Stochastic Calculus and Financial Applications**, New York (Springer-Verlag).

Stephens, M., 2000, Convergence in European Mortgage Systems before and after EMU, in: **Journal of Housing and the Built Environment 15** (1), pp. 29-52.

Talaga, J.A. and J. Buch, 1998, Consumer Trade-off among Mortgage Instrument Variables, in: **International Journal of Bank Marketing 16** (6), pp. 264-270.

Templeton, W.K., R.S. Main and J.B. Orris, 1996, A Simulation Approach to the Choice between Fixed and Adjustable Rate Mortgages, in: **Financial Services Review 5** (2), pp. 101-117.

Trigeorgis, L., 1996, **Real Options: Managerial Flexibility and Strategy in Resource Allocation,** Cambridge (Mass.) (MIT Press).

Toussaint, J. and M. Elsinga, 2007a, The Netherlands: Positive Prospects and Equity Galore, in: Elsinga, M., P. de Decker, N. Teller and J. Toussaint (eds.), **Homeownership beyond Asset and Security: Perceptions of Housing related Security and Insecurity in eight European Countries,** pp. 173-200, Amsterdam (IOS Press).

Toussaint, J. and M. Elsinga, 2007b, Homeownership and Income Security, in: Elsinga, M., P. de Decker, N. Teller and J. Toussaint (eds.) Homeownership beyond Asset and Security: Perceptions of Housing related Security and Insecurity in eight European Countries, pp. 287-312, Amsterdam (IOS Press).

Tucker, M., 1991, Comparing Present Value Costs Differentials between Fixed and Adjustable Rate Loans: A Mortgage Simulation, in: **Financial Review 26** (3), pp. 447-458.

Turner, B., R. Kreft and Z. Yang, 2005, **Security aspect of Homeownership: a microanalysis**, Uppsala (www.osis.bham.ac.uk, accessed 07 November 2006).

Tversky, A. and D. Kahneman, 1992, Advances in Prospect Theory: Cumulative Representation of Uncertainty, in: **Journal of Risk and Uncertainty 5** (4), pp. 297-323.

Vose, D., 1996, **Quantitative Risk Analysis: a guide to Monte Carlo simulation modelling**, Chichester (John Wiley & Sons).

Weintraub, E. Roy, 2002, **How Economics became a Mathematical Science**, Durham (Duke University Press).

Wilmott, P., 2001, **Quantitative Finance**, Chichester (John Wiley & Sons).

Whitley, J., R. Windram and P. Cox, 2005, **An Empirical Model of Household Arrears**, working paper no. 214, London (Bank of England).

Wolswijk, G., 2005, **On some fiscal effects on mortgage debt growth in the EU**, ECB working paper no. 526, Frankfurt (ECB).

Wong, J., L. Fung, T. Fong and A. Sze, 2004, **Residential Mortgage Default Risk in Hong Kong**, Hong Kong Monetary Authority.

Yang, T.T., H. Buist and I.F. Megbolugbe, 1998, An Analysis of the Ex-ante Probabilities of Mortgage Prepayment and Default, in: **Real Estate Economics 26** (4), pp. 651-676.a

Appendix A **Estimation of the interest and income model**

A. Estimation of the interest model

Here I followed the approach suggested by Chen *et al.* (1995). Recall,

$$(1) \quad dr_t = \lambda(\mu - r_t)dt + \sigma\sqrt{r_{t-1}}\, dX$$

Recall that λ is the speed of adjustment of the actual interest r_t to the long-term mean μ, and $\sigma\sqrt{r_{t-1}}$ is the implied volatility. The values of are dr_t normally distributed (Cox *et al.*, 1985) with a mean and variance of:

$$E[r_t|r_0] = r_t e^{-\lambda t} + \mu(1-e^{-\lambda t})$$

$$V[r_t|r_0] = r_t\left(\frac{\sigma^2}{\lambda}\right)[e^{-\lambda t}-e^{-2\lambda t}]+\mu\left(\frac{\sigma^2}{\lambda}\right)[1-e^{-2\lambda t}]$$

Note that the variance is a function of the dependent variable r_t, i.e. it is time-dependent. This automatically leads to a more complicated estimation procedure for the different variables. A weighted least square regression analysis is necessary (Judge *et al.*, 1982). First, a simple regression model can be estimated:

$$r_t = \beta_0 r_{t-1} + \beta_1 + \xi_t$$

$$\beta_0 = e^{-\lambda t} \wedge \beta_1 = \mu(1-e^{\lambda t})$$

Here, the error term ξ_t is no longer identically and independently distributed (since it depends on time); therefore, ordinary least squares do not apply. With the variance structure specified above, however, we can see this as a regression model with heteroskedasticity. Therefore, since the variance of the error term is equal to

$$E[\xi_t^2] = r_t\left(\frac{\sigma^2}{\lambda}\right)[e^{-\lambda t}-e^{-2\lambda t}]+\mu\left(\frac{\sigma^2}{\lambda}\right)[1-e^{-2\lambda t}]$$

a second regression model may be estimated:

$$\xi_t^2 = \omega_0 r_{t-1} + \omega_1 + s_t$$

$$\omega_0 = \left(\frac{\sigma^2}{\lambda}\right)[e^{-\lambda t}-e^{-2\lambda t}] \wedge \omega_1 = \mu\left(\frac{\sigma^2}{\lambda}\right)[1-e^{-2\lambda t}]$$

The results of the first regression model can be used for solving λ and μ, and the results of the second for σ. The results are shown in Table A.1.

The data used consist of monthly data from 1990:1 to 2004:12. For the euro-countries, the 1-month AIBOR/EURIBOR interest rate was used; for Denmark and the UK respectively the 3-months deposit rate, DKK and the end month sterling Interbank lending rate, mean LIBID/LIBOR.

Table A.1 Estimation of the interest model: the results

	Belgium	Denmark	France	Italy	Netherlands	UK
Mean-reversion level μ	0.0390	0.0440	.	.	.	0.0450
Implied volatility $\sigma\sqrt{r_{t-1}}$	0.0410	0.0330	.	.	.	0.0460
Reversion speed λ	0.2395	0.2801	.	.	.	0.3834
Spread (av.)	0.0100	0.0070	0.0050	0.0150	0.0040	0.0110
Market price of risk	-0.0358	0.0217	.	.	.	0.0255

The market price of risk was estimated by comparing yield-curves in January 2004 and minimising the sum of squares difference of the estimated and actual yield-curves.

B. Estimation of the income model

Here, I follow closely the approach suggested by Dutta et al. (1997). Recall:

$$(2) \quad \begin{bmatrix} \text{Prob.} & \theta & dy_t = \mu dt + \sigma dX_2 \\ \text{Prob.} & (1-\theta) & dy_t = \tilde{y}_t / y_{t-1} \end{bmatrix}$$

in which the new household income $\tilde{y}_t$ is drawn from the distribution $N(\tilde{\mu}_t, \tilde{\sigma}_t)$ with $\tilde{\mu}_t$ and $\tilde{\sigma}_t$ as the mean and variance of the recurrent distribution. So, what we need is to estimate the model $\Gamma = (\mu, \sigma, \theta, \tilde{\mu}, \tilde{\sigma})$. The income in any year is the outcome of a dynamic process in which the household income changes from year to year depending on the economic cycle and economic events and demographic transformations.

The mean and variance of the income in year $t+1$, conditional on household income in year t, are:

$$M(y_{t+1}|y_t) = \theta(\mu + y_t) + (1-\theta)\tilde{\mu}$$
$$V(y_{t+1}|y_t) = \theta\sigma^2 + (1-\theta)\tilde{\sigma}^2 + \theta(1-\theta)(y_t + \mu - \tilde{\mu})^2$$

in which $y_t = \log(y)$. The parameters $\Gamma = (\mu, \sigma, \theta, \tilde{\mu}, \tilde{\sigma})$ can be estimated by maximising the conditional likelihood:

$$L(yt, \Gamma) = \sum_{i=1}^{N} l_t(y_t, \Gamma) = \ln\phi\left[\frac{y_{t+1} - M(y_{t+1}|y_t)}{\sqrt{V(y_{t+1}|y_t)}}\right] - \frac{1}{2}\ln(V(y_{t+1}|y_t))$$

in which $\phi[.]$ is the standard normal density function.

In the original study by Dutta et al., different alternatives for θ were assessed. Besides the linear variant presented above, θ was estimated as a function of income and/or for different subgroups depending on age and/or education. Here, I experimented with different specifications for θ. For most countries, a breakdown of θ into two income groups – θ_h and θ_l – proved most appropriate. Therefore, the final estimated model was $\Gamma' = (\mu, \sigma, \theta_h, \theta_l, \tilde{\mu}, \tilde{\sigma})$.

Dutta et al. (2001) constructed their model based on the personal income of the head of the household. This study, however, accords prime importance to the household income as such and not to the income of individual members. The model considers this by including the income of all the household members with the age of 18+. Note that net income is more volatile at the house-

Table A.2 Estimation of the income model: the results

	Belgium		Denmark		France	
Coefficients						
Kappa (*low income group*)	0.8960		0.8550		0.8650	
Kappa (*high income group*)	0.6470		0.4650		0.6340	
Mean (*non-mover*)	0.0160		0.0050		0.0238	
Implied volatility (*non-mover*)	0.0453		0.0395		0.0280	
Mean (*mover, log*)	10.3780		10.6270		10.3510	
Volatility (*mover, log*)	0.0690		0.0550		0.1970	
	Predicted	*Observed*	*Predicted*	*Observed*	*Predicted*	*Observed*
Mean	10.25	10.25	10.51	10.51	10.25	10.25
Standard deviation	0.33	0.39	0.27	0.35	0.32	0.40
N		3,406		3,655		5,967
R^2		0.757		0.727		0.753
	Italy		**Netherlands**		**UK**	
Coefficients						
Kappa (*low income group*)	0.9030		0.7310		0.8380	
Kappa (*high income group*)	0.7890		0.5370		0.6210	
Mean (*non-mover*)	0.0177		0.0146		0.0103	
Implied volatility (*non-mover*)	0.0222		0.0198		0.0155	
Mean (*mover, log*)	10.0280		10.2990		10.3120	
Volatility (*mover, log*)	0.2010		0.0870		0.2650	
	Predicted	*Observed*	*Predicted*	*Observed*	*Predicted*	*Observed*
Mean	9.93	9.92	10.24	10.24	10.11	10.11
Standard deviation	0.36	0.42	0.16	0.29	0.41	0.51
N		6,157		8,688		6,428
R^2		0.781		0.574		0.714

The results show that the model captures the underlying income changes rather well. Since the standard deviation is for all countries lower than in the observed series, income uncertainties seem to be underestimated. The model fit for the Netherlands is relatively poor; i.e. 43% of the yearly income changes are not accounted for in the model.

hold level than at the individual level due to, amongst others, demographic factors (e.g. divorce).

Finally, the estimation was performed with the ECHP panel dataset for the period 1995-2001. The results are shown in Table A.2.

Appendix B Optimal mortgage choices under different conditions

In section 5.3 the costs and risks are evaluated of different mortgage types in different countries given the differences in the underlying institutions and characteristics of homeowners. This appendix presents a partial analysis of different features of both, showing how the different conditions interfere with optimal mortgage choices. The partial analysis covers six different scenarios:
1. The baseline scenario
2. A scenario in which the mortgage interest tax relief system is abolished
3. A scenario in which repossession time is extended
4. A structural increase in inflation
5. A structural increase in real interest rates
6. Finally, a scenario presenting optimal choices for low-income households.

The calculations of all six scenarios are based on the paradigmatic case representing the recent buyers in the Netherlands. The same analysis could be performed mutatis mutandis for other countries. Given the differences in the baseline scenarios, the outcomes would be different, but the direction of the shift in the optimal mortgage choice would be the same (e.g. with a systematic increase in inflation, long-term mortgages with variable interest rates are more beneficial).

The costs and risks of different mortgage types[68] are (re)calculated under the above-mentioned six scenarios. For each different scenario, the optimal mortgage in terms of lowest costs, lowest risks are presented in Table B.1.

A detailed discussion of the various outcomes is not required here. However, it is worth noting that the results show significant differences in the optimal mortgage choice under different conditions. Implicating those households concerned should alter their mortgage choice when conditions changes for the reason that their present mortgage renders suboptimal. By adjusting their mortgage choice, borrowers may save money and/or reduce risk. To give one example: an abolishment of the much debated mortgage interest rate facility in the Netherlands will lead to an initial rise in costs of €69,433. On the other hand, changing the mortgage choice towards the new optimum (see Table B.1) will lead to a decrease in expected cost of ~€26,000; hence, just by adjusting mortgage choices households could save 38.6% of the initial increase following an abolishment of the mortgage interest tax relief system (Neuteboom, 2008).

Overall, the results show that the optimal mortgage choice (mix) for individual homeowners changes for the different scenarios. On a more aggregate level it shows, once again, that differences in mortgage take-up (outcomes) across countries do not necessarily imply a fundamental difference in the underlying household decision making process. That is, if changes in institu-

---

68 See the set of mortgage types defined and shown in Table 5.1.

Table B.1 **Optimal mortgage choices under different conditions (recent buyers in the Netherlands, 2003)**

| | Base scenario | Institutional changes | | Economic conditions | | |
		Mortgage Interest Tax Relief abolished	Repossession Period extended ½y → 5y	Structural increase in Inflation +1%	Structural increase in Interest +1%	Household with lower income
Lowest risks	Interest-only mortgages with short duration and variable interest rates	Serial mortgages, 20-year duration, fixed interest rate period	Interest-only mortgages, 20-year duration with variable interest rate	Serial mortgage, 20-year duration and 10 years with variable or fixed interest rates, closely followed by interest-only mortgages	Serial mortgage with short duration and fixed interest rate	Savings mortgage, 30-year duration with variable interest rate
Lowest costs	Savings mortgages, 30-year duration, 10 years to variable interest rates	Investment mortgages, 20-year duration, 10 years fixed, closely followed by serial mortgages	Serial mortgage with fixed interest rates and long duration	Long duration, especially interest-only mortgage with variable interest rate	Savings mortgage with 30-year duration and variable interest rate	Serial loan, 30-year duration, 10 years fixed, closely followed by a savings mortgage with long duration and fixed interest rate

This table shows the optimal mortgage choice a homeowner should opt for, if acting rational. The abbreviations in each cell corresponds to mortgage type, fixed interest period and total duration (see the different assessment categories in Table 5.1).

tions and/or economic conditions occur, the optimal mortgage shifts. Hence, in a cross-country analysis in which by definition both economic conditions and institutions differ – not withstanding growing European cooperation – the optimal mortgage differs accordingly.

Over rationeel gedrag van leners

Een vergelijking van de risico-attitude van eigenaar-bewoners

By Peter Neuteboom
Summary (in Dutch)

Eigenwoningbezit mag zich in Nederland en daarbuiten verheugen in een grote, en groeiende, populariteit. Omdat het merendeel van de(ze) eigenaar-bewoners niet in staat is de aankoop van een eigen huis geheel uit eigen middelen te financieren, betekent deze trend eveneens dat het hypotheekbezit[69] onder eigenaar-bewoners de afgelopen jaren sterk is gegroeid. Momenteel bedraagt de uitstaande hypotheekschuld in Europa €5,1 biljoen (EU15, 2005), dat wil zeggen meer dan 40% van alle uitstaande bankkredieten en gelijk aan ruim een derde van het gezamenlijke bruto binnenlands product. Binnen Europa verschilt het hypotheekbezit echter aanmerkelijk, zowel op micro- als macroniveau.

Die uitstaande, en groeiende, hypotheekschuld is een toenemende bron van zorg voor financiële autoriteiten in binnen- en buitenland; daarbij wordt expliciet verondersteld dat de uitstaande schuld een goede indicator is van de risico's die huishoudens, de financiële sector en de economie als geheel lopen. Meer impliciet blijft dat de uitstaande hypotheekschuld ook iets zou zeggen over de risicohouding (= attitude) van eigenaar-bewoners; dat wil zeggen dat een hoge hypotheekschuld 'suggereert' dat het betrokken huishouden bereid is meer risico's te lopen.

In dit proefschrift worden beide noties ter discussie gesteld. Risico's van hypotheken zijn immers complex en veelzijdig waarbij veel exogene en endogene factoren van invloed zijn, factoren die ook nog eens sterk tijd- en plaatsgebonden zijn. Dit noopt tot een zorgvuldige en consistente 'vertaling' van hypotheekbezit naar kosten en risico's; noodzakelijk om de werkelijk risico's van hypotheken voor eigenaar-bewoners te kunnen identificeren en vergelijken.

Ten minste drie factoren maken dat hypotheekgebruik door eigenaar-bewoners niet direct kan worden begrepen als indicator voor de onderliggende risico's, zeker in een internationale vergelijking. Allereerst gaat het hierbij om de relevante institutionele context (regelgeving, subsidies, sociale zekerheid, arbeidsmarkt etc.). De institutionele context beïnvloedt mede de oorzaken, de aard en omvang van de risico's van hypotheken voor huishoudens. Zo kan bv. een goed sociaal vangnet de gevolgen van inkomensonzekerheid/werkloosheid voor huishoudens (gedeeltelijk) wegnemen; en betekenen royale fiscale randvoorwaarden (o.a. hypotheekrenteaftrek) dat de werkelijk kosten van een hypotheek aanmerkelijk kunnen worden teruggedrongen. Daarnaast is het ri-

---

69 Dit begrip slaat op zowel de omvang van de hypotheekschuld als de (gangbare) financieringsvormen.

sicoprofiel van (potentiële) eigenaar-bewoners niet gelijk. In het ene land representeert het landelijke gemiddelde ook een gemiddelde eigenaar-bewoner; in andere landen vindt er een uitsortering plaats waardoor de rijkste en/of meest kansrijke huishoudens in de eigenwoningsector zitten. Daardoor kunnen deze laatste, ondanks een hogere hypotheekschuld toch minder risico's lopen. Ten slotte zijn, ondanks verregaande Europese samenwerking, hypotheekmarkten nog steeds primair nationale markten. Met onder meer als gevolg dat het palet aan hypotheken waaruit eigenaar-bewoners kunnen kiezen, en de risico's die daarmee samenhangen, uiteenlopen tussen landen.

Dus, hoewel, in termen van hypotheekbezit er onder huishoudens in Europa grote verschillen bestaan, kan a priori dus niet worden verondersteld dat de verschillen in hypotheekgebruik binnen Europa synoniem zijn met verschillen in risico's en risicohouding. Verschillen in institutionele context en kenmerken van kopers en nationale hypotheekmarkten hebben grote invloed op de werkelijke netto kosten en risico's van het hypotheekbezit.

De rationele keuze theorie veronderstelt dat huishoudens kiezen voor het voor hen meest gunstige alternatief (hier: hypotheek). Indien onzekerheid bestaat over de risico's die samenhangen met de verschillende alternatieven, hangt de uiteindelijke keuze van huishoudens af van hun individuele risicohouding. Gegeven het gewicht van de woonuitgaven (hypotheekkosten) binnen het totale beschikbare huishoudbudget mag worden verondersteld dat huishoudens overwegend risicomijdend zijn. De centrale hypothesen in dit proefschrift weerspiegelen deze verwachting: (I) huishoudens kiezen overwegend rationeel en (II) huishoudens zijn daarbij primair risicomijdend (hoofdstuk 1).

In hoofdstuk 2 worden de concepten risico en risicohouding bediscussieerd. Risico's worden in dit verband gedefinieerd als een combinatie van onzekerheden, kansen en negatieve consequenties. In het hoofdstuk worden onzekerheden – waarmee huishoudens rekening (zouden) moeten houden – verkend (zie hiervoor); evenzo de mogelijke negatieve consequenties voor hen (bv. betalingsproblemen of gedwongen verkopen). Ten slotte wordt een conceptueel model uitgewerkt waarmee de risicohouding van huishoudens kan worden gemeten en vergeleken tussen landen.

De overeenkomsten en verschillen in hypotheekgebruik, de institutionele context, evenals de karakteristieken van (potentiële) eigenaar-bewoners en van nationale hypotheekmarkten worden beschreven en bediscussieerd in hoofdstuk 3. De focus ligt hierbij op ontwikkelingen in België, Denemarken, Frankrijk, Italië, Nederland en het Verenigd Koninkrijk. Deze analyse toont aan dat er grote verschillen bestaan tussen de verschillende landen; een eenduidige rangorde kan echter niet worden vastgesteld, omdat de verschillende relevante aspecten te veelzijdig zijn en daardoor niet eenduidig vallen te vergelijken.

De resultaten vormen de noodzakelijke achtergrond voor de interpretatie van de resultaten van deze studie ten aanzien van risico's en risicohouding.

Om de kosten en risico's van hypotheken eenduidig in beeld te brengen is een simulatiemodel ontwikkeld (hoofdstuk 4). De belangrijkste elementen van de relevante institutionele context zijn hierin gemodelleerd, evenals de kenmerken van huishoudens en van specifieke hypotheekvormen. Omdat zowel de kenmerken van huishoudens (bv. het inkomen), als de kosten van de gekozen hypotheek veranderen in de tijd (door bv. inflatie of rentewijzigingen) is een meer dynamische aanpak noodzakelijk, waarbij de totale kosten van de hypotheek over een lange periode worden berekend. In het model wordt daar rekening mee gehouden door de huizenprijzen, inkomen, rente, inflatie en aandelenkoersen als endogene variabelen te beschouwen. Aldus kan het feitelijke hypotheekbezit van eigenaar-bewoners worden 'getransformeerd' naar de werkelijke kosten en risico's die dit voor hen impliceert.

Het model kan ook worden gebruikt om de risicohouding van huishoudens te meten (hoofdstuk 5). Deze risicohouding wordt afgeleid door de gekozen hypotheek(vorm) van een eigenaar-bewoner te vergelijken met alle alternatieven die voor hem open staan. Omdat de kosten en risico's deels afhankelijk zijn van individuele omstandigheden en van de relevante institutionele context, is het daarbij wel noodzakelijk dat de vergelijking plaatsvindt op basis van een consistente output indicator, dat wil zeggen de kosten en risico die aan een dergelijke keuze verbonden zijn.

De resultaten van de analyse worden gepresenteerd en bediscussieerd in de hoofdstukken 4 en 5. Op basis van de resultaten gepresenteerd in hoofdstuk 4 kan de conclusie worden getrokken dat de kosten en risico's die aan specifieke hypotheekcontracten gekoppeld zijn, sterk verschillen tussen landen. De gemiddelde kosten – over de gehele looptijd van de hypotheek, in netto contante waarde – die aan een standaard hypotheek van €100.000 kleven, lopen uiteen van €113.000 in Nederland tot meer dan €147.000 in het Verenigd Koninkrijk. De risico's van hypotheken – onzekerheid over de totale omvang van de toekomstige betalingen, betalingsproblemen of gedwongen verkoop – variëren evenzeer. Hierbij zijn de risico's slechts gedeeltelijk proportioneel met de omvang van de kosten an sich, deels ook gekoppeld aan de hypotheekvorm. Deze resultaten tonen aan dat in een internationale vergelijking, simpele indicatoren zoals de uitstaande hypotheekschuld weinig zeggen over de daadwerkelijke risico's voor huishoudens, de financiële sector en/of de overheid.

In hoofdstuk 5 wordt de risicohouding van huishoudens verder geanalyseerd. Zoals mocht worden verwacht – op grond van de rationele keuze theorie – blijkt uit de analyse dat huishoudens ondanks alles toch 'uitkomen' op een hypotheek die gegeven hun persoonlijke omstandigheden en de institutionele context waarbinnen zij moeten kiezen (nagenoeg) optimaal is; dat wil zeggen dat huishoudens in de onderzochte landen overwegend rationeel kiezen. Daarnaast blijken huishoudens in de onderzochte landen overwegend risicomijdend te zijn. Dat wil zeggen dat zij opteren voor alternatieven met een laag risicoprofiel. Huishoudens in het Verenigd Koninkrijk blijken relatief het meest risicozoekend te zijn; hoewel de verschillen substantieel zijn, kiezen zij ook niet coûte que coûte voor de hypotheek met de laagste kosten. Ook als nader wordt ingezoomd op specifieke groepen – zoals starters, jongeren en lage inkomensgroepen –, verandert het beeld niet wezenlijk. Met andere woorden: beide hypothesen worden bevestigd door het onderhavige onderzoek.

Ten slotte, de belangrijkste implicaties van het onderzoek zijn:

1. Woningmarkten zijn complexe markten, waarbij veel factoren directe en indirecte invloed uitoefenen op de markt als geheel en op de positie van de verschillende deelnemers. Om dit adequaat te ondervangen, zal in internationaal vergelijkend onderzoek het accent moeten verschuiven van een meer beschrijvende analyse naar het nauwkeurig(er) in beeld brengen van de impact van beleid en (economische) condities op de positie van de verschillende partijen. Kwantificering is daarbij onontbeerlijk, zoals onder meer de resultaten van deze studie hebben aangetoond (voor wat betreft de risico's en risicohouding van kopers).

2. Financiële autoriteiten, in binnen- en buitenland, zullen moeten investeren in betere indicatoren om (nationale) hypotheekmarkten te monitoren. De analyse toont aan dat de risico's die samenhangen met het hypotheekbezit – om verschillende redenen – tussen landen sterk uiteenlopen. Gevolg is dat de grote aandacht voor landen met hoge uitstaande hypotheekschulden (bv. Nederland en het Verenigd Koninkrijk) niet in verhouding staat tot de risico's die deze positie met zich brengt voor de financiële markten. En omgekeerd, in landen met een lage uitstaande schuld (bv. Italië) zijn de risico's voor individuele eigenaar-bewoners en de financiële sector veel groter dan op grond van de relatieve omvang van de hypotheekschuld mag worden verwacht.

Curriculum vitae

Peter Neuteboom was born in Zoetermeer on October 9, 1960. In 1979 he obtained his VWO diploma from the Erasmus College in Zoetermeer. He holds a Msc. in Economics from the Erasmus University in Rotterdam, where he graduated in 1985. Afterwards he worked in different positions at the Dutch Ministry of Housing, Spatial Planning and the Environment, before returning to the University-world again (challenged by doing a PhD-research). He joined Delft University of Technology, OTB Research Institute for Housing, Urban and Mobility Studies, in 2000.

Part of the research of this thesis was presented earlier at venues in Germany, Switzerland, Spain and the UK. Earlier versions of the model, presented in Chapters 4 and 5, were published in the Journal of Housing and the Built Environment and the European Journal of Housing Policy; several related papers are under review.

Nowadays he holds a dual position as a researcher at Delft University of Technology and at RSM Erasmus University Rotterdam.

Sustainable Urban Areas

1. Beerepoot, Milou, **Renewable energy in energy performance regulations. A challenge for European member states in implementing the Energy Performance Building Directive**
   2004/202 pages/ISBN 90-407-2534-9 (978-90-407-2534-0)
2. Boon, Claudia and Minna Sunikka, **Introduction to sustainable urban renewal. CO$_2$ reduction and the use of performance agreements: experience from The Netherlands**
   2004/153 pages/ISBN 90-407-2535-7 (978-90-407-2535-7)
3. Jonge, Tim de, **Cost effectiveness of sustainable housing investments**
   2005/196 pages/ISBN 90-407-2578-0 (978-90-407-2578-4)
4. Klunder, Gerda, **Sustainable solutions for Dutch housing. Reducing the environmental impact of new and existing houses**
   2005/163 pages/ISBN 90-407-2584-5 (978-407-2584-5)
5. Bots, Pieter, Ellen van Bueren, Ernst ten Heuvelhof and Igor Mayer, **Communicative tools in sustainable urban planning and building**
   2005/100 pages/ISBN 90-407-2595-0 (978-90-407-2595-1)
6. Kleinhans, R.J., **Sociale implicaties van herstructurering en herhuisvesting**
   2005/371 pages/ISBN 90-407-2598-5 (978-90-407-2598-2)
7. Kauko, Tom, **Comparing spatial features of urban housing markets. Recent evidence of submarket formation in metropolitan Helsinki and Amsterdam**
   2005/163 pages/ISBN 90-407-2618-3 (978-90-407-2618-7)
8. Kauko, Tom, **Between East and West. Housing markets, property prices and locational preferences in Budapest from a comparative perspective**
   2006/142 pages/ISBN 1-58603-679-3 (978-1-58603-679-9)
9. Sunikka, Minna Marjaana, **Policies for improving energy efficiency in the European housing stock**
   2006/251 pages/ISBN 1-58603-649-1 (978-1-58603-649-2)
10. Hasselaar, Evert, **Health performance of housing. Indicators and tools**
    2006/298 pages/ISBN 1-58603-689-0 (978-1-58603-689-8)
11. Gruis, Vincent, Henk Visscher and Reinout Kleinhans (eds.), **Sustainable neighbourhood transformation**
    2006/158 pages/ISBN 1-58603-718-8 (978-1-58603-718-5)
12. Trip, Jan Jacob, **What makes a city? Planning for 'quality of place' The case of high-speed train station area redevelopment**
    2007/256 pages/ISBN 978-1-58603-716-1

13. Meijers, Evert, **Synergy in polycentric urban regions. Comple-mentarity, organising capacity and critical mass**
2007/182 pages/ISBN 978-1-58603-724-6

14. Chen, Yawei, **Shanghai Pudong. Urban development in an era of global-local interaction**
2007/368 pages/ISBN 978-1-58603-747-5

15. Beerepoot, Milou, **Energy policy instruments and technical change in the residential building sector**
2007/238 pages/ISBN 978-1-58603-811-3

16. Guerra Santin, Olivia, **Environmental indicators for building design. Development and application on Mexican dwellings**
2008/124 pages/ISBN 978-1-58603-894-6

17. Van Mossel, Johan Hendrik, **The purchasing of maintenance service delivery in the Dutch social housing sector. Optimising commodity strategies for delivering maintenance services to tenants**
2008/283 pages/ISBN 978-1-58603-877-9

18. Waterhout, Bas, **The institutionalisation of European spatial planning**
2008/226 pages/ISBN 978-1-58603-882-3

19. In preparation

20. Pal, Anirban, **Planning from the bottom up. Democratic decentralisation in action**
2008/126 pages/ISBN 978-1-58603-910-3

21. Neuteboom, Peter, **On the rationality of borrowers' behaviour. Comparing risk attitudes of homeowners**
2008/112 pages/ISBN 978-1-58603-918-9

Copies can be ordered at www.dupress.nl.